Communications Technology and Democratic Participation

Kenneth C. Laudon

The Praeger Special Studies program—
utilizing the most modern and efficient book
production techniques and a selective
worldwide distribution network—makes
available to the academic, government, and
business communities significant, timely
research in U.S. and international economic, social, and political development.

Communications Technology and Democratic Participation

PRAEGER SPECIAL STUDIES IN U.S. ECONOMIC, SOCIAL, AND POLITICAL ISSUES

Praeger Publishers   New York   London

Library of Congress Cataloging in Publication Data

Laudon, Kenneth C   1944–
    Communications technology and democratic participation.

    (Praeger special studies in U.S. economic, social, and
political issues)
    Includes bibliographical references.
    1.   Political participation—United States. 2. Com-
munication in politics—United States.   3. Democracy.
I. Title.
JK1764.L38   1977   320   77-7471
ISBN 0-03-021836-5

PRAEGER SPECIAL STUDIES
200 Park Avenue, New York, N.Y., 10017, U.S.A.

Published in the United States of America in 1977
by Praeger Publishers,
A Division of Holt, Rinehart and Winston, CBS, Inc.

789   038   987654321

Printed in the United States of America

ACKNOWLEDGMENTS

The research reported here was supported by a National Science Foundation (NSF) grant to the Center For Policy Research (Project #GI-29940) during the years 1970-72.

I would like to thank Professor Amitai Etzioni (Department of Sociology, Columbia University, and Director of the Center) and Dr. Stephen Unger (Department of Engineering, Columbia University), who were the principal investigators for the NSF project, for their generous support. In particular, Amitai provided wise counsel and advice in the early stages of the research design, and read several versions of the manuscript.

In addition, I would like to thank Professor Alan Westin (Department of Political Science, Columbia University), who read the final version of the manuscript at a critical moment. Alan's keen understanding of the issues involved in the relation of technology and society contributed enormously to the final manuscript.

Equally important to the background of this work is the contribution of the 10,000 members of the League of Women Voters of New Jersey, who participated in the field experiment reported in Chapter 4. Nearly 10,000 questionnaires were completed by League members, and some in panel studies graciously completed three questionnaires over a period of several months. I would like to thank the then president of the League, Nina McCall, for opening the organization to social scientists, and for allowing experimentation with the League's decision-making process.

I have also benefited from the intellectual and administrative skills of Ms. Sara Lipson (Ph.D. candidate, Columbia University) who carried the brunt of organizing the field study on a limited budget.

In the preparation of this manuscript for publication, several chapters of empirical analysis were either deleted or condensed. Some of this material appears in Chapter 4, but the great bulk was eliminated for the sake of brevity and to allow room for material of broader interest. Readers interested in greater quantitative analysis should consult the final report of the NSF project. In addition, the raw data is available from the Center For Policy Research.

CONTENTS

Chapter   Page

LIST OF TABLE AND FIGURES

1

INFORMATION TECHNOLOGY AND POLITICAL DEMOCRACY

With the availability of greatly expanded electronic communication facilities, better access with less delegation of authority could be provided. With a more informed public and with the possibility of automatic opinion sampling or voting, a much greater degree of direct participation at all levels of government would be available. . . . It could lead to great social understanding and greater access to and transfer of information, while improving the opportunities for both freedom and privacy!

J.L. Holt, "Cheap Communications," *The Futurist*, 1969

The United States has lived the future to escape the present. New technologies replace the open plains and encourage a discount of the present for perfect futures. In the United States these futures involve, alternatively, the emergence of a rationally governed society, and the arrival of social and political equality. Together these dreams bind over the wounds of a corrosive reality neither rational nor egalitarian. Each in its time, the developments of steam energy, electricity, telephones, radio, television, and, even more so, recent developments in computers and telecommunications have sparked new hopes for rapid attainment of these dreams. In the United States the messiah is technology.

This is not a study of the future, but rather an examination of present social and technological forces which are sufficiently powerful to define a future for political democracy in the United States. This future involves the idea that through innovations in telecommunications it is possible to restore to citizens and their organized groups a measure of political power and skills sufficient to countervail the mega-institutions that surround them. We shall call this the vision of citizen technology.

Plans and actual experiments in citizen technology began to appear in the late 1960s. They vary considerably, depending upon the technology used and organization. Some call for automated national and regional polling, accomplished by computer reading of citizen preferences punched into voting boxes attached to a home telephone; direct access to political decision makers via two-way cable television, with citizens indicating their preferences by punching numbered keys on a home voting box; or, in truly futurist visions, by speaking directly to decision makers. With these plans, a national referendum involving millions of voters could take place in hours. Other plans call for the use of satellites to connect smaller groups of like-minded citizens separated by great distances; the use of neighborhood cable television to narrowcast the hopes and plans of neighborhood leaders directly to constituents. In New York City, the experiment involves the opening up of cable studies for direct public access to permit mobilization of popular support by activist groups, wired cities and buildings to allow broadcasting from one home to many, or narrowcasting from one home to another. With all these plans the ability of citizens to form more powerful coalitions and groups than heretofore possible with grass-roots organizations becomes feasible.

Citizen technology is then the promise of a renewal of democracy, more accountable elites, a less alienated and more active citizenry. It is also the threat of a new telefascism made palpable by the realization of one astute observer that "there is no difference between the electronics that make demagogy easier and those that make responsible politics easier."[1]

The groups involved in shaping this odd marriage between populism and advanced technology form a pageant of Americana: entrepreneurial tinkerers; hermaphroditic alliances of social scientists and engineers; giant monopolies in broadcasting, telecommunications, and computers seeking to preserve their share of an unknowable market; new and smaller firms in cable television, data transmission, and peripheral equipment seeking any profitable use of their wares; government regulators hoping to preserve a dubious past; and handfuls of politicians skeptical of citizen technology and others supporting it to show the electorate they care.

A movement is quietly gaining momentum to give democracy a technological fix. It is spurred by federal research and development grants that have totaled nearly $50 million since 1968 and much larger outlays by private industry in cable television, data transmission, satellites, and peripheral hardware. Keeping pace, bit by bit, the technological hardware is appearing: new buildings with prewired cable television here, automated telephone polling devices there, computer-assisted conference-calling devices, design and tests of digital two-way cable television in small communities, regional experiments with an "electronic town hall", and pilot studies of the use of remote terminals connecting citizens directly with government computers to permit citizens to test out the consequences of public policy decisions before voting for specific proposals.

The interest in a citizen technology is not without a profit motive. The communications technology envisaged in many plans for citizen technology can be used to sell products directly to the consumer in his home, including individualized education services; respondent lists of national referenda can be sold to direct mail advertisers; commercials can be tested out in regions of the country with consumers responding rapidly to market researchers. More directly, the owners of the technology itself, as well as the providers of home voting boxes, display terminals, and other equipment, stand to make a profit.[2]

These commercial implications of citizen technology in turn have potentially far-reaching social consequences. Further development of a "cashless" society becomes feasible with a broad expansion of two-way communications technology. Other consequences include substantial deurbanization, in which communication is substituted for travel to and from work, and information utilities providing direct access to libraries. With less need for cities as cultural centers, one planner sees a marked drop in crime. Another, less modest than most, is "exploring the possibility of changing the whole ecology of human settlement by providing rural areas by telecommunications with the cultural and social amenities of urban life."[3]

"CAN TECHNOLOGY CLEAN THESE AUGEAN STABLES?"

The lure of citizen technology cannot, however, be reduced to hidden profit motives or desires for broad social change per se, even though these factors are important to the motivations of many corporations and planners. Mounting interest among social scientists, engineers, and computer scientists in citizen technology is largely due to a deep, growing fear of recent sociopolitical trends in the United States and a sober pessimism about efforts in the 1960s to change U.S. society and its government.

Among the more disturbing trends in political life are the long-term growth in affluence and education coupled with a doubling of alienation from democratic institutions in the last decade; a 50 percent decline in the ability of institutional elites (from the military to education) to engender public confidence in the same period; the patent corruption of basic institutions, from political parties to large business, coupled with a dwarfing of the average individual vis-a-vis these institutions made ever more powerful through centralization, new management techniques, and spare cash.[4]

An IBM engineer organizing a conference for the Institute of Electrical and Electronic Engineers on the potential of the new citizen technology for revitalizing democracy typifies the views of corporate and public planners:

> The elected representatives of the people are viewed as *them* rather than *us*. Sometimes alienation of portions of the public from government tends to be the most prominent feature of their attitudes. . . .

Many of the operations of government, even at the municipal level, are conducted in an atmosphere of self-serving secrecy. . . . The widespread use of one-way broadcast channels of communication makes the manipulation of public opinion relatively easy; and it makes dialog relatively difficult.

The economics of two-way teleconferencing communications is particularly attractive where the density of users is high. Thus, there is also reason to hope that new technology will alleviate some of the ills of urban political life.[5]

The fear of current trends in political life is strengthened by the belief that unless something is done to regain a sense of legitimacy for U.S. institutions, the society will crumble before a wave of new demagogues. And, in considering how this new legitimacy is to be attained, the efforts toward social and political change in the last 15 years hold some bitter lessons.

THE NEW INTELLECTUAL CONSERVATISM

The attractiveness of citizen technology derives not only from the pessimism over current affairs, but also from a heightened awareness that two major efforts at societal change have failed in the last decade and a half. The first was a resurgence in the early 1960s of U.S. populism and the idea that citizens could take effective direct action against large institutions. The second effort, a few years later and continuing to this day, was that advanced computer information systems could make government more rational, effective, and responsive to social needs. Throughout U.S. history, populism and the progressive themes of improved management alternate and interact. They spring from widely held sentiments that some kind of change is needed to preserve the republic.

The new populism of the 1960s rekindled the myth of direct citizen action based on passionate involvement of ordinary people, now elevated by sheer spirit to the status of decision makers and capable of altering the direction of society. Beginning with the civil rights movement and culminating in the antiwar movement of the late 1960s, the new populism engaged a broad spectrum of Americans from the poor and minority groups to wealthy scions of suburbia. It was largely and inherently a populist movement devoid of bureaucratic expertise, corporate sponsorship, high technology, and thus of organizational sophistication. Impaled on the thorns of political opposition and weariness of participation, the movements were denied their ultimate goals of a more egalitarian and democratic sodiety at peace with the world. The new populism, as with past experiences, seems to have tragically underestimated the enormity of the undertaking and the strength of opposing institutions.

Simultaneous with the movements of the 1960s, though far less publicized, was a rebirth of the progressive ideal of rational government. Here social problems are reduced to managerial problems amenable to solution by fine tuning the bureaucratic apparatus. Tied to advances in computer design, with significant corporate sponsorship and the blessing of political approval, the movement of advanced information systems into public government continues at a brisk pace. Yet here, too, there is growing recognition that the ultimate goal of this effort—a more rationally managed, effective, and responsive government—is no more than a distant dream. As we describe later, the hopes for an expert democracy sustained by a scientific managerial elite have become obscured by continued irregularity, fragmentation, and inequity in the management of public affairs.

The failure of these experiments in social change, taken together, forms the support for a new intellectual conservatism. The social policy journals, popular magazines, and books of the early 1970s reflect an abdication of many liberal intellectuals from the tasks of social reform. In its place are prescriptions for the old medicine: ignore a social problem and it ceases to be social. Increasingly we are exhorted to place our faith in the nineteenth century marketplace. If welfare rolls grow too rapidly in one city, cut back support levels, and recipients will either find work or go to some other city with higher support levels. If the poor need more housing, then destroy what they have and replace it with factories. The homeless and penniless will move to other locations, based on self-interest, and better housing filled with higher-income individuals will replace the old. If crime is rising among the young, then increase the certainty of punishment, and age the young like wine. Often the proposals of the new conservatism are couched in the obscure language of systems analysis (purporting to reflect a systematic and empirical analysis of all the factors relevant to a social problem). Appropriately, these proposals are proclaimed by their sponsors as "counter-intuitive," or lacking common sense.[6]

THE MARRIAGE OF POPULISM AND TECHNOLOGY

The first concrete plans and experiments in citizen technology began appearing not long after computers entered government in the middle 1960s. This is roughly the point at which cable television was recognized to hold great potential (both commerical and other) for urban areas. The novel aspect of citizen technology is its reliance on advanced information technology and its populist ethos. It is in some respects a synthesis of the two preceding, yet failed, social experiments. It is a sort of people's technology, which has the potential for strengthening grass-roots or populist organizations into coherent and powerful coalitions via telecommunications. If citizens were allowed greater scrutiny of public officials, public policies would be more responsive, and vice versa, permitting leaders to lead more effectively by strengthening their contact with citizens.

Hence, for many the idea of citizen technology is a powerful palliative to the current pessimism and reaction generated by the immediate past. Solid advances in telecommunications and information technology make it more than an empty promise.

THE TECHNOLOGY

Central to our analysis of citizen technology is a family of information technologies developed in the last two decades, the most important of which are computers organized into large-scale information systems, and new telecommunications devices linking computers, institutional decision makers, and by extension, the larger public to both of the former.

Progress in the art of storing, processing, and transmitting information is difficult to measure precisely because two factors are involved: the growth in sheer numbers of machines and installations, and the growth in the capacity of machines to handle information. Both factors have changed dramatically in the last two decades.

From a handful of electronic computers in the 1950s the total number of installations in the United States has grown to about 109,000. Federal government use has grown from 2 in 1950, to 400 in 1960, and to 5,300 in 1970. State governments have increased usage from less than 100 installations in 1960 to more than 500 in 1970 (not counting the 750 higher-education installations).[7]

Number counts of installed computers hide changes in capacity over this same period of two decades; latest third-generation computers possess several million times the storage capacity of early computers and perform the task several thousand times faster. Moreover, the penetration of computers into the society is much greater than implied by the above figures. The use of time-sharing programs in which many users are connected via telecommunications to a single computer servicing hundreds of remote terminals is perhaps a better indicator of computer use. There is now one data terminal for every 100 civil servants in the United States—eight times more than in 1970; there are 2 such terminals for every 100 service sector workers, indicating greater penetration of computers in the private sector. Currently there is 1 terminal for every 200 Americans (a tenfold growth in 5 years), and by 1980 the number will double. At this growth rate, sometime in 1990 there will be as many data terminals per capita in the United States as there were telephones in 1970 (56 per 100 citizens).[8]

Yet these figures do not convey any sense of the social impact of computers on industrial societies, which one writer characterizes as the transition from an industrial to an information society, where the "dominant labor activity is information processing rather than industrial production."[9] Dividing the labor force into industrial, agricultural, information-processing, and service sectors, the same author calculated the percentage of persons working in information-processing occupations to be near 50 percent in 1975 (roughly double what it was in 1960). Others have found that by the mid-1960s over 30 percent of the national economy was devoted to the production and distribution of information.[10]

Increasingly the distinction between telecommunications and computers becomes harder to maintain. Not only have new data-transmission technologies such as cable and microwave extended the role of computers, but computers also play a larger role in controlling and expediting the flow of information through telecommunications facilities. The most advanced and extensive of such systems is the Electronic Switching System (ESS) of American Telephone and Telegraph. In 1965, AT&T began a $1 billion investment program designed to totally automate telephone exchanges. Previously, connecting one party to another was accomplished with electromechanical relays. In 1965, these were replaced with semiautomatic systems operating ten times faster and far cheaper than the old circuits; in 1975 these, in turn, were being replaced with totally automated message centers run by a single computer, which quadruples the message-handling capacity from 150,000 to over 550,000 calls per hour, using half the electricity. The ESS system also allows four dialers to set up their own conference calls, with groups of up to 30 possible through special arrangement. By squeezing more and more calls into existing cable and microwave transmission circuits, the cost of long-distance telephoning has been kept at 1953 levels in constant dollars.[11]

CABLE

It is clear that further extension of these trends toward greater information handling and processing ability will rely upon the continued improvement in telecommunications devices which can link users in remote places to computers and can allow computers to connect remote terminal users to one another rapidly. Here lies the significance of coaxial cable. Compared to telephone wire, which is a twisted pair of light copper wires, small coaxial cable has a core of much larger dimensions (about one-eighth of an inch) and an outer braided wire cover; the two conductors are insulated from one another and covered with a plastic wrapping. Coaxial cable has about 300 times the data-carrying capacity of telephone wire, or as engineers like to refer to these matters, about 50,000 bits per second in some systems (a "bit" of information is a coined word from *binary digit* and refers to either a 0 or 1) depending upon the size of the cable. As the average large computer works at a speed of about 1 million bits per second, it is clear that a substantial limitation on the growth of an information society will be the capacity of links between computers and users.[12]

A major use of cable is the long-distance transmission of exchanges between computers, largely business. In 1970 there were 14 billion such transactions in over 3.7 billion data calls.[13]

Yet even more significant for our work is the use of cable to carry television signals and information to the home. In broadcast television using radio signals, about 13 channels which have good technical qualities can be utilized. With cable, 40 to 80 channels are possible without interference. Anywhere from 20 to 40 two-way channels are possible, which would allow the home user to talk with a central studio, or with proper engineering, to call on demand anyone else with similar two-way ability, just like a phone call. Of course, cable television is much different from a phone call: pictures can be transmitted, books can be ordered from the library and copied on a home printer, food and other goods can be purchased, and one can utilize the services of a central computer to figure out one's taxes. Briefly, then, the message-carrying ability of cable is quantumly higher than that of a simple telephone wire. Indeed, any one of the above activities would completely tie up a local telephone exchange if more than 100 people were involved. With cable, the information tasks of millions of city residents can be accommodated.

The growth in computers, microwave data transmission, and cable distribution systems is what many have aptly called the "information revolution." Engineers, who have a penchant for counting things, now estimate that the computers in the United States alone have an active memory capacity equal to one-tenth of the world's books (about $.9 \times 10^{14}$ bits of information), not counting all the information stored on computer tapes and cards. With 40 billion Xerox-electrostatic copies being made each year now (compared with only 9 million published book pages), it would seem the end of the age of Gutenberg is upon us. Even if we admit, as we must, that much of the information stored, copied, and transmitted is unorganized gibberish (the distinction between knowledge and information is lost upon computer engineers), the gains have been impressive.[14]

Moreover, the acceleration of change in information processing appears to be up, not down, as the following table compiled by Ithiel Poole illustrates:

Ages of Communication Media

Medium	Age in Years
speech	500,000
writing	4,000
archives	2,000
printing	500
telegraph	140
typewriter	110
radio	50
TV	25
computer	25
Xerox	20
satellite	10

As Poole points, out, even our knowledge about the social uses and impact of information is obsolete: the vast part of our knowledge about mass communications is based upon early market research from the age of radio and television.[15]

ELECTRONIC DEMOCRACY: DOES THE TECHNOLOGY EXIST?

The vision of citizen technology is the extension of democracy through electronic means. Many of the plans we discuss below envisage electronic town halls in which citizens, from the sanctity of their private homes, can directly confront their leaders and also persuade their fellow countrymen. These fantasies are currently far beyond the communications potential of existing technology. They would require a replacement of existing phone wires with much higher cable capacity. The estimated cost of rewiring the nation in such a manner is currently about $1.2 trillion. Even if a smaller scale is considered, such as suburban towns near high density cities, the costs of simply laying cable are extremely high: $10,000 per mile for suburbs, and in New York City $75,000 per mile.[16]

In the United States, responsibility for the development of public communications has been given under license to private corporations. This holds true not only for radio, television, and telephone, but also for new technologies like cable and satellites. It is unlikely this pattern will change in the near future, and therefore, the future of a rewired cable nation upon which many dreams for a citizen technology rest will depend largely upon the profitability of commercial cable television. Political use of cable, in other words, will have to be "piggybacked" onto commercial systems. Indeed, much of the regulation of cable television by the Federal Communications Commission (FCC) and local authorizing agencies has attempted to do just this.

Yet the future of cable television is far less bright than during the mid-1960s when industry spokesmen predicted half the nation would be wired with cable by 1977. The reasons for the failure of cable to reach more than 10 percent of the nation's homes in 1977 are both financial and institutional.

The cable industry began in 1950 with the establishment in Lansford, Pennsylvania, of the first commercial cable television station. The industry has grown from 800 systems serving 850,000 subscribers in 1962 to 2,700 systems serving 6 million subscribers in 1977—about 10 percent of the national television audience. Its principal use is to provide clear signal reception from distant or weak broadcast stations. In the top 100 markets, some original programming is done, although far less than FCC regulations call for. Yet the fivefold growth in cable subscriptions has largely ceased in the 1970s.[17]

The demise of the cable fable, a "wired nation," resulted from a conflict between communication technologies and the institutional forces behind them. Cable had three enemies: over-the-air broadcast industry, telephone companies, and print media—newspapers, publishing, and magazines. Together, these groups have effectively limited the program content of cable systems in the top 100 television markets (where the action and growth is). In 1966, under pressure from broadcasting sources, the FCC prohibited cable from importing distant signals to the top 100 markets unless it could prove it did not damage existing broadcasters. In 1968, the FCC strengthened this by forcing cable operators to obtain permission from the program originator in a distant town for each program imported. As the ownership of cable stations changed to include many large equipment manufacturers and broadcasters, and under pressure from civic groups and municipalities in top markets to unleash cable, the FCC ruled in 1971 that cable could import to major markets some programs without prior permission. Even here, the programs could not violate the "exclusive rights" clause, which allows a broadcaster to buy exclusive rights to, say, a movie for several years and thereby prevent its being shown in that market. Moreover, cable systems cannot "leapfrog," that is, import signals into Washington from New York without importing programs from closer markets like Pittsburgh.[18]

Limitations in program content and distribution imposed by the FCC and demanded by broadcasters are not the only hurdles facing cable. Local municipalities that license cable systems also have imposed a heavy burden. In New York City, for instance, the two cable systems were required to install free public access studios and channels, provide three governmental channels, produce shows of local origination, and by 1975 develop a capacity for neighborhood programming where signals could be limited to local communities. New York City cable operators have lost money for four years, and growth in subscriptions has all but ceased.

CITIZEN TECHNOLOGY: THE PROSPECTS

It is clear to observers of cable that one-way cable systems will predominate through the 1980s and that their growth will be considerably slower than earlier predicted. Their development will depend not so much on technology as on changes in institutional alignments. Two-way cable television is envisaged as likely for the 1990s and is dependent upon far-reaching social changes, such as the replacement of travel to shopping centers by home shopping services, the transformation of libraries from fourteenth century reading rooms to program and facsimile originators, and growing demands for home computer services.

The institutional barriers to the growth of cable television are enormous. For those fearful of a rampant technology's shaping society in its interests, cable television stands as a massive counter example, the direction of which is determined by "a requirement to accommodate a distorted institutional structure supposedly created because of the particular characteristics of past technologies," as one critic of the FCC comments.[19]

While cable television has failed to live up to early predictions because of institutional resistance, the current strength of that resistance appears to be weakening. Put another way, cable television is gaining in strength, in part because of local business and governmental interests, which have much to gain by taking the shackles off cable TV. A recent report of the House Communications Subcommittee has branded FCC regulations as an "improper, unconstitutional and illegal umbrella against competition." Among the benefits of cable cited in the report is "the unusual ability of cable television to provide two-way communication [which] means it can be used to show customers merchandise in their homes and then permit them to order it." Not to slight the humanitarian benefits, the report also suggests that "cable can be used to enable teachers to have conversations with shut-in students."[20] Joining in the attack against FCC regulation of cable, the antitrust division of the Department of Justice has recently filed a brief in the United States Court of Appeals (District of Columbia) arguing that the current rules are not justified "in terms of an immediate need to protect public interests."[21]

With an executive branch opposed to federal regulation as a matter of principle, and with growing support among local business and governmental leaders, the future of cable is less negative than critics suggest. If the legal barriers are removed, extensive one-way cable systems are likely by 1980, and large, commercial two-way cable systems are probable by 1990.

THE PROBLEM

To be sure, the full-blown "wired nation" fantasy of citizen technology is years off. Equally sure, however, is that in the lifetime of most readers, a combination of commercial, technological, and political forces will produce several close approximations to the fantasy. Moreover, it seems clear to many that continued reliance upon nineteenth century techniques of citizenship is unlikely to preserve democracy into the twenty-first century.

The question before us, then, is not when will the technology arrive, but rather how might we organize the technology to enhance democracy without at the same time destroying its most valued features. To avoid this question now is to relinquish important social and political questions to private corporations and electronic engineers.

Along these lines, we want to ask: Should citizen technology be organized to strengthen the bonds between political leaders and citizens as many suggest, or should it focus instead on strengthening the bonds between citizens and their organized groups? The technology required and its organization is quite different, as are the political consequences.

Should the purpose of citizen technology be to reduce the psychological "sense of alienation" among citizens or, rather, should its purpose be—to borrow a phrase—to increase the political "throw weight" of organized citizens? How might the latter be accomplished, and the mass participatory therapy sessions, which are envisaged by some, avoided?

Assuming that citizen technology can be organized in such a manner as to give citizens more actual political influence, what is to prevent the emergence of a plebiscitarian democracy, a sort of mob rule? How might we preserve a necessary amount of discretion for political leaders and a reasonable, full deliberation of issues which allows even unpopular views to be heard? In short, we must ask if a citizen technology can be designed in a manner that would not destroy the checks and balances that have been built into democracy for good reason.

THE POLITICAL ECONOMY OF INFORMATION

Assuming the technology could be designed and organized in such a manner as to strengthen democracy, the next question is, given the way U.S. society actually is (warts and all), who would actually utilize the new technology and who would benefit? This question is more complicated than it appears because, as noted above, citizen technology will most likely emerge as a useful adjunct to a multiservice system. The same cable that attempts to strengthen your political influence will also provide channels to buy groceries, receive the latest government white paper, and clear your checking account. The technical system of which citizen technology would be a part clearly will benefit banks, private corporations, and other groups selling their wares. Indeed, these commercial and governmental functions are the only conceivable way citizen technology could be paid for in the United States.

But let us put these other considerations aside for the moment and look at the political benefits and costs. One question that arises is the compatibility of the ethos of populism and advanced technology. Is it possible to marry populism to an advanced technology largely not understood or controlled by the people who use it? Can the face-to-face, highly personal recruitment tactics of social movements work with cable television or telephone conference calls? More to the point, would Martin Luther King have been as effective on television? Would Allen Ginsberg be able to levitate the Pentagon by remote control as he attempted to do in person in 1968? Or would the broad acceptance of citizen technology spell the end of populist action as it has existed in our history? Worse, controlled by powerful monopolists and regulated by federal administrators, would not the new technology be in fact a telefascism of pseudoparticipation, easily supervised and sanitized by the same forces of domestic intelligence that brought us the White House horrors?

Looking at the broad range of organizations in the United States with differing commitments to internal democracy, from large private corporations, on the one hand, to Mayor Daley's political machine, or the radical mayor of Madison, Wisconsin, and then to consumer action groups, which of these kinds of organizations would desire or benefit from greater democratization of their organizations? Is the idea of an electronic democracy emphasizing an active citizenry compatible with the managerial ethos of U.S. organizational life, which emphasizes efficiency, hierarchy, and centralization? Reversing historical trends toward the rule by a few or oligarchy, would a citizen technology be able to bring democracy to the internal life of modern organizations, or rather, would it be ignored or perhaps used by these organizations to reinforce their hegemony? As the average adult American spends most of his waking hours enmeshed in an ever more articulate management structure, these are not unimportant questions.

An even broader set of questions involves the relationship between the new information technology (of which citizen technology is a part) and historical patterns of social and political inequality in the United States. Assuming equal access to citizen technology for all groups of citizens, is there anything to suggest it would in fact be used equally by all groups?

What we know about the so-called information explosion of the last decade is that everyone's level of information increases, but for some persons and groups it increases faster than others. Studies of public libraries, "Sesame Street," and educational television show that, even under conditions of free and equal access, the wealthy and skilled groups of society increased their levels of information faster than the poor and unskilled.[22] New information technologies, then, are likely to increase the information gap that currently exists among important groups in the United States.

This finding becomes especially important in the discussion of a new information technology, which has direct political consequences. Would the new citizen technology be used primarily by the upper-middle class, educated, and active citizens organized in diverse groups from Nader Raider clubs to ecology action corps? Is the technology likely to create new social and political communities where none existed before among the poor, uneducated, and inactive? Or would citizen technology only mirror the existing inequalities and, in some instances, if the past is a guide, increase the gap?

PLAN OF THE BOOK

We have, then, two questions to answer. The first is, How ought citizen technology be designed and organized to strengthen democracy? The second is, How, in fact, is it likely to be used, given the nature of U.S. society? The answers will be sought in four different ways. First, in the remainder of this chapter we shall critically review the actual experiments and proposals for citizen technology developed in the last five years. Second, we shall seek to establish the requisites of democracy in large national states like the United States, and illustrate how citizen technology could be designed to enhance attainment of these requisites. This will involve organizing technology to fit the nature of democracy, not vice versa.

Familiar with what has been done in the field and with the outlines of a more appropriate fit between technology and democracy, we shall then test these ideas in a field experiment. The field experiment uses a large, democratic organization of about 10,000 members as a vehicle to further explore problems in the design and operation of citizen technology in a realistic setting. With this experience we can begin to answer the last question: What role will a citizen technology, in all likelihood, play in U.S. society?

THE FIT BETWEEN INFORMATION TECHNOLOGY AND DEMOCRACY

Before beginning a review of current plans and experiments with citizen technology, it is necessary to illustrate briefly the relation between a technology, its mode of organization, and its social or political consequence. The point we wish to make is quite simple: implicit in the development of certain information technologies are very definite models of democracy which differ considerably from one another.

Consider, for instance, three new information technologies: the computer used in your local welfare department, the automated telephone conference call which allows ten or more community leaders to have a telephone meeting, and audience "feedback" shows used by National Educational Television (NET) to allow viewers to call in their response to controversial issues. These contemporary technologies are closely related. Each involves new ways of collecting, storing, transmitting, and displaying information; each depends on similar post-World War II electronic devices such as transistors, cathode ray tubes, computer switching, and "reading" of telephone votes; each portends, with continued development, to heighten the role of information in modern society and thereby to affect critical areas of social life such as privacy, public decision making, the nature of work and authority, and perhaps even the form of community.

Yet these technologies are members of three rather different families of information technology. The basis of distinguishing among these technologies is largely social: each affords different kinds of people the opportunity to communicate with one another and, in general, to use information.

Data-Transformation Technology

The computer belongs to a family of information technologies that could be labeled "data-transformation technology": it serves as a tool for the collection, storage, manipulation, and retrieval of very large information pools. What we know about the social organization of computers is that, due to their immense cost, only very large institutions such as agencies of the state or private corporations can own or lease them. Within this larger institutional framework, it is also clear that an advanced degree in one of the physical or social sciences is required to use a computer. (About 1 percent of the population has such advanced training; of these, only perhaps one in ten has any facility with the computer. We do not count here, of course, the small businesses, professionals, and others who use computer billing services or are billed by computers. Their inclusion here would only distort the meaning of the word *use*.) The mode of organizing the computer is therefore one of expert access to and control of information flows.

The political impact of computers as they moved decisively into the public sector during the 1960s—which is what concerns us here—was clearly to enhance the role of experts and systems analysts in public affairs. The political model of democracy which sprang from these events and was touted by leading computer firms and intellectuals of the time is best described as the managerial model of democracy. As discussed later in this chapter, it is a model of democracy in which feedback from social reality to government computers would be so rapid, accurate, and detailed, policy alternatives and outcomes so clearly defined and rationally weighed by a scientifically trained elite, that there really would not be much point in active citizen participation in government.

It is conceivable, but extremely unlikely, that changes in computer technology will lead to widespread access to computers. The vision of a "computer in every pot" is, however, largely a fantasy of flabby futurism. Even if large computers in the future became as accessible to the average person as, say, cheap pocket calculators, it seems highly unlikely that the average noncollege-educated citizen would be able to use them with as much effect as the managerial decision makers of the state or large institutions. To expect otherwise is to contradict most of what is known about who actually uses and benefits from current advances in information technology.

Mass-Participation Technology

A second family of information technologies with quite different principles of organization and political consequences is what might be termed "mass-participation technologies." This would include the traditional broadcast media (radio and television), one-way cable television (even neighborhood cable systems), and other mass media that function to transmit information from one central source to thousands or millions of persons. It would also include those technologies that work in reverse, from millions to one central location, such as opinion polls, government complaint centers established in some urban areas, radio call-in shows, automated vote-tabulating machines which automatically count the preferences of thousands of citizens as they call stations. Most of the current plans and experiments with citizen technology employ these kinds of devices, which are reviewed later.

The central fact about these technologies is that the average citizen can possess some aspect of the technology: a television or radio, plus the amount of literacy and intelligence requisite to respond to a message. When a direct response is elicited, here, too, the average person can be given the means of response: a mail-in opinion survey, a telephone to call the station or, in some futurist views, a little box that is attached to the television cable and records the viewers' preferences in the central studio. Given the cheapness and widespread distribution capable with these technologies, the mode of organization can be called plebiscitarian. That is, it allows direct access between elite groups in society and average citizens without mediation by other institutions.

The model of democracy called forth by mass participation technology is best called "populist." Aided by the development of new electronic devices, the new electronic populism is a model of democracy in which interest in public affairs could be made so intense, and widespread, detailed, technical information about complex political issues so broadly disseminated and understood, and the preferences of millions of active citizens instantaneously recorded, that there really would not be a need for experts, elites, or intermediary institutions— such as political parties or Congress—except as discussion moderators. The new populism based on recent advances in mass participation technology from opinion polls to television call-in show vote tabulators is then the virtual direct opposite of expert democracy.

Interactive Technologies

The third family of information technology we will call "interactive." This would include the most widespread interactive device, the ordinary telephone, and also operator-assisted telephone conference calls (which allow up to 30 persons to "meet" over the phone and discuss issues) and automated conference telephone calls (which currently allow four persons to meet together from their homes without operator assistance). Also included here would be recent technologies such as two-way cable systems, interactive computer networks which allow computer terminals (and their operators, presumably) to contact each other, as well as point-to-point microwave television transmitters which currently allow 17 local governments of the New York City Metropolitan Region to have live monthly "electronic" meetings on shared problems.

The interesting special difference with interactive technologies is that they allow for horizontal communication flows among individuals and organized groups on a regular basis. The other technology families are largely vertical communication devices: computers allow experts to collect and centralize information about citizens, and the mass media technologies allow a small group of persons to broadcast to millions. Interactive technologies allow, on the other hand, ordinary citizens to talk with one another; or allow, in the case of conference calls, organized groups like tenant association leaders to discuss issues and plan actions—in short, to communicate with like-minded people and groups on demand. None of the other technologies permit this kind of com-munication flow.

Not a great deal is known about how the more advanced interactive technologies are socially organized or will be in the future. Of course, a great deal is known about personal telephone calls: they are used to communicate with like kinds of people—friends, family, colleagues, and so forth. By and large, personal telephone calls follow social status lines in the United States, occurring predominantly within subgroups of social class, ethnicity, relition, neighborhood, and so on. Our experience with larger-scale interactive tech-nologies is more limited. Telephone conference calls, although a technical possibility for over 30 years, are not advertised and hence not used, largely because AT&T believes it does not make money on such calls; the newer auto-mated four-person conference calls are only recent innovations and similarly are not made readily available for cost reasons. Futuristic two-way cable systems, which would be similar to a telephone with picture added, simply do not exist in large enough numbers to permit hard and fast conclusions.

Yet some characteristics of social organization for advanced interactive technologies like wide-scale conference calling (either with telephones or cable) are suggested by current personal telephone use and by the very nature of the technology. In the first instance, access to the technology is currently wide-spread: just about anyone can use the telephone for a conference call. In the future, it is likely that there will be in use two-way cable systems which would allow the home viewer to participate in neighborhood meetings from his home. In this sense, access to a large part of the technology is not so severely restricted as with computers.

Yet clearly, the advanced interactive technologies are more restricted in their use than mass-participation technologies like ordinary television or opinion polling. To use a conference call requires some organizational skill: other partic-ipants to a conference call meeting must be contacted beforehand; data, agenda, and billing arranged; and the phone company must be notified of all partic-ipant names and numbers. Use of this kind of technology requires, therefore, a higher interest threshold than, say, turning on the television. It requires also the commitment of time and energy far greater than responding to an opinion poll. In terms of access and control of information flows, then, interactive technologies currently (and likely in the future) will be used largely by pre-existing organized interest groups, that is, those groups that have the requisite skills, interest, and commitment to use the technology. The predominant mode of organizing interactive technology can thus be termed "subgroup organization." This means, of course, that the Big Three auto makers will (and curently do) use interactive technologies for business planning and decision making. It's cheaper than flying around the country to various meetings. However, given the simplicity of the technology and the likelihood of more innovations in this area, interactive technologies can also be used by a variety of much smaller grass-roots types of organizations, such as local ecology groups, consumer groups, block associations, political clubs, and a host of "single issue" groups active in U.S. politics.

The model of democracy implicit in the use of interactive technologies is best termed "pluralist." In this view, a more widespread dissemination of existing interactive devices, such as telephone conference calls, and a judicious development of new two-way cable television would enhance the ability of local organized groups to reach agreement with one another on public policy issues, to plan strategies of political action and, in general, to strengthen the organizational potential of heretofore isolated and disorganized local groups in the United States vis-a-vis the more powerful, institutionalized power blocs that dominate the political landscape. This new pluralism implicit in interactive technologies is thus neither a promise of instant citizen action along the lines of electronic populism nor a continuation of expert paternalism. What is new about this pluralism is the attempt to make pluralism of the old sort work: that is, an organization of power in which interest groups of roughly equal organizational capacity compete for political support in a variety of legitimate ways to shape public policy.

The use of interactive technology such as conference calls to enhance an existing democracy is the focus of our experiment in Chapter 4. The relations between a technology, its modes of organization, and implicit model of democracy are summarized in the table below:

TABLE 1

Relationship between a Technology, Its Modes of Organization, and Implicit Model of Democracy

Technology Family	Typical Mode of Organization	Implicit Political Model
Data transformation Computers	Expert guidance	Managerial democracy
Interactive Conference calls	Organized sub-groups	Pluralism
Mass participation Broadcasting Opinion polls	Plebiscitarian	Populism

Source: Compiled by the author.

The point of making these observations is not to argue for a broad conception of technological determinism. On the contrary, our position is that technology is a facilitating factor that interacts with existing historical, organizational, and environmental pressures to shape the future. Yet, it is also clear that certain technologies facilitate some goals better than others, and work to the advantage of some conceptions of the future rather than others. In the case of the various families of information technology described above, a variety of factors involving economics, size, state of the art, and expertise suggest that each technology imposes restrictions on who has access to the information potential and who controls its flow—what we call "the mode of organization." When looking at the political implications of information technology in a democracy, these differences in access and control lead to differences in who benefits and who loses influence, who decides to participate in what decisions, when, and how.

Recognizing these differences among technologies, we can avoid a technological determinism. The danger is that simply because progress is made in one technology (often at the expense of another) our conception of democracy changes to accommodate the requisites of that technology. The case of public-sector computer use provides us with a recent historical experience of just such a danger.

THE FATE OF MANAGERIAL DEMOCRACY

From World War II to perhaps 1960, U.S. political commentary focused on two related questions: what were the sources of facism, and what are the elements of an enduring democracy? The heroes of this intellectual enterprise were typically small, organized groups of citizens banded together in vocational, professional, business, labor, and even leisure groups. This Jeffersonian melange of autarchic free groups provided significant protection for the ordinary citizen: the state could not monopolize his life, membership filtered the mass media message through several layers of small group leaders, and, not least of all, these groups allowed citizens to develop their own opinions and plans to shape governmental policy. (See Chapter 3.) The villains were an all-powerful bureaucratic state on the one hand and populist demagogues on the other. Lurking in the background was the threat of a mass society (one with few organized groups) which theoretically made demagoguery possible and the totalitarian-bureaucratic state inevitable.

Beginning in 1960 with the publication of Daniel Bell's article, "The End of Ideology in the West," and extending to about 1970, the subject of political commentary shifted radically to a concern with rationality in the management of public affairs, order, technicism, and in general a love affair with expertise.[23] The origins of this shift are mulitple. In part the shift was due to a growing belief expressed by Bell that the "uncritical application of ambient ideas from European sociology to the vastly different experiences of American life" was simply inadequate to describe the reality or potential future of the United States; the old European problems—and theories—of communism, socialism, and social class were foreign to the U.S. experience.[24] In part also, the shift was due to an even more important recognition that the old ideologies offered few, if any, solutions to pressing U.S. concerns: civil rights protests, urban decay, then riots, then war, and finally, antiwar rebellion. The old "marxillac," a word one writer coined for the problem, just wasn't what she used to be.

In the absence of other events, this might have been just a further sign of the intellectual ennui abundant in the late 1950s. But the hundredfold increase in computer use by the federal government during the 1960s and similar advances in local government, coupled with even more impressive growth in information handling capacity of the new computers, provided the age when ideology ended with new heroes, villains, and a sense of drama to match most European ideologies.

The new vision of this period was variously described by its supporters as the "technetronic society," one increasingly being shaped by technology and electronics (Zbigniew Brzezinski), or, similarly, the "postindustrial society," an axial principle of which was "the centrality of theoretical knowledge as the source of innovation and of policy formulation for the society" (Bell); for its detractors, the new vision became a "technostructure embracing all who bring specialized knowledge, talent, or experience to group decisionmaking" (John Kenneth Galbraith).[25] One point the detractors and supporters all believed: the new computing machines, the professional groups of experts arrayed about the machines, and the newly developed techniques of decision making employed by these experts, were now in effective control of the key social institutions from private enterprise to the state.

The political implications of these analyses augured for rather different views of democracy than those discussed since World War II. The active citizens, organized into small, plural, Jeffersonian groups, literally disappear as a grounding for public policy. In their place is a new elite of scientifically trained state managers; in place of an authentic consensus of the governed, the new prop of legitimacy is functional rationality. According to Bell:

> The rise of the new elites based on skill derives from the simple fact that knowledge and planning—military planning, economic planning, social planning—have become the basic requisites for all organized action in a modern society. The members of this new technocratic elite, with their new techniques of decision-making (systems analysis, linear programming, and program budgeting), have now become essential to the formulation and analysis of decisions on which political judgments have to be made, if not to the wielding of power. It is in this broad sense that the spread of education, research, and administration has created a new constituency—the technical and professional intelligentsia.[26]

The new heroes, then, of the managerial democracy become members of the educational and scientific estate who alone, in the words of Galbraith, will have the knowledge, independence, and foresight to make the new society both rational and humane:

> It is to the educational and scientific estate, accordingly, that we must turn for the requisite political initiative.
> The initiative cannot come from the industrial system, although support can be recruited from individuals therein. Nor will it come from the trade unions . . . they are under no particular compulsion to question the goals of the industrial system. . . .[27]

Indeed, the future of democracy could no longer be sustained by ordinary citizens and nineteenth century autarchic groups. The ever more complex world—a phrase exhausted by true believers in futurism—required, in Brzezinski's words, a "grand reentry [of academia] into the world of action . . . stimulated by the growing involvement in national affairs of what Kenneth Boulding has called "the Educational and Scientific Establishment (EASE)."[28]

And who were the new villains? In the context of managerial democracy they turn out to be the organized interest groups, which in previous years were thought of as the very stuff of democracy. Indeed, the villians could be found all over the political map, and were variously described as parochial interests, "old machine politicians," industrial-era vested interests, for example, labor, and "counterculture" groups who not only refused to join the team but did not even believe in science. Likened by Brzezinski to the nineteenth century European reaction to the Industrial Revolution, "not quite certain where it was heading—yet sensitive to the miseries and opportunities it was bringing," the contemporary opponents of the new managerialism were unlikely to develop any solid base of support, thus were relegated to the status of romantic anachronisms. Yet if they did develop a base of internal support, in a "last spasm of the past," they could be suppressed quickly through "continuous surveillance over every citizen . . . containing even most personal information about the health or personal behavior of the citizen, in addition to more customary data. These files will be subject to instantaneous retrieval by the authorities."[29] So much for the buzzing, blooming confusion of U.S. politics once thought to be its greatest asset. This would have to be sacrificed, paraphrasing John Stuart Mill, to the further perfection of the machinery of the state.

THE GRAND REENTRY

We now know the grand reentry of scientism into the public sector fizzled somewhere in the upper atmosphere from whence it came. The sense of failure is in part due to the absurdly high expectations that intellectuals placed in the new information technology, often without any firsthand knowledge of its actual state of development. Like Marx, who saw in the "cyclopean steam engines" of nineteenth century England the ultimate liberation of man from

work, the modern political commentator was all too easily lured into the utopian fantasies created nowadays by computer firms, government agencies, bureaucrats, and other academics similarly misinformed.[30] The sense of failure is heightened more directly by the obvious evidence of failed results: the so-called think-tank war in Vietnam, bankrupt cities, growing inequality, recession, and not least of all, the perversion of the Constitution accomplished through massive "national security" intelligence data banks. Briefly, federal domestic social policy associated with expert advice and advanced information systems—from school busing to expensive, regional rapid-transit systems—did not fare well in the late 1960s and early 1970s.

Yet the actual sources of the failure of managerial democracy are more complex than simple technological false consciousness, a problem of heightened expectation on the part of a few intellectuals, or the failure of a few large federal programs. Indeed it was at the local levels of government where the most intense efforts and expenditures on the advanced new computer technology occurred. Here the hope was to change fragmented, departmentalized filing systems into massive, machine-readable, centralized files enabling city and county officials to deal "more effectively with the complex and dynamic urban environment."[31] With the development of social indicators for housing, transportation, health, and employment, it was thought possible to develop solutions for problems before the cities burned to the ground. That a few cities did burn in the late 1960s only strengthened the arguments of the new urban managers for the development of management information systems.

Today, from the Santa Clara County, California, Local Government Information Control system (LOGIC) to the New Haven Urban Management Information System (UMIS), the landscape is fairly littered with the rubble of an explosion in managerial technology. Largely restricted now to the mundane data storage and retrieval needs of line agencies, the computer's current role is that of an electronic clerk—admittedly a very big and efficient clerk, but a clerk nonetheless.

To those who have observed these systems into the mid-1970s, it appears that the failure of the computers to bring about any real or interesting change in public policy or its administration is chiefly due to the fundamental misconception that local governments are miniuniversities desirous of tinkering with and altering public policy to suit the latest feedback from the computer. By and large, the politicans for whom the experts worked were not, after all, interested in management information systems that might produce unpopular public policy. This meant the computers could be used in an effort to make the police-arrest function more efficient (that was popular with just about everyone) but would not be used to ferret out judicial corruption by tracing major felons through the courts, and would not be used to argue for massive expenditures in corrections, parole, or rehabilitation (these were not popular with anyone and never have been). In welfare, computers were publicly ballyhooed as a bulwark against welfare cheats (vast storehouses of information were kept on clients) but were not used to collect data on service providers who own the Medicaid mills and nursing homes for the elderly or on the professionals who work therein.[32]

Once the interest groups that comprise the U.S. governmental enterprise mobilized control of the new computer technology, whatever capacity it may have had for "rationalizing government was lost. As it turns out, that capacity was never very large to begin with: social systems are incredibly more complex than physical systems. Given the highly limited nature of social science knowledge, it was not possible to translate the total systems view of computer experts from the space program into public life without significant distortions. The end result is the current reality of computers used by municipal, county, and state governments in the routine collection of mundane administrative data.

It would be wrong to conclude that in this limited role computers have been inconsequential. They have brought a measure of rationality and sanity to the budgeting procedures of local and state governments. The consequence of not using computers in the budgeting process is illustrated by New York City, whose budgeting maze rivals mythology for its numerous pitfalls, laws, and minor deities. A recent analysis in 1976 turned up over 500 separate accounts for the activities of one agency, the Board of Education. Following the recent financial crisis, even New York will develop a modern computerized accounting system which is supposed to "scrap such abuses as grossly exaggerated revenue inflow, procrastinated expenditure charges, hidden and "negative balance" accounts, and fictitious Federal and state aid claims—all habits of the city's discredited status quo."[33]

It is too early to know if the leprechauns of Tammany Hall can be so easily defeated. Experience elsewhere indicates that something more than good bookkeeping is required to bring felicity to urban areas. Rather than providing any hope for a revolution in the management of urban affairs, the real legacy of experiments in managerial democracy is an efficient reproduction of the historical conflicts, inequities, and fragmentation of public policy.

SOME LESSONS

The point of this brief sketch of managerial democracy is not to chronicle the depths of intellectual narcissism that computers gave rise to, but rather to extract from this recent experience some perspectives that will aid us in the discussion of more recent experiments and proposals for a citizen technology.

The first perspective is that technologies do not have an impact upon societies like some giant supertanker grounding on a stormy coast. Often lost in popular tracts discussing the so-called impact of technology is the notion, widely shared by those who have looked closely at the phenomenon, that technological change is filtered through extant social values, ideologies, and interest groupings.

A second, related perspective is that technologies do not alter the direction of a society, but rather facilitate existing trends. Technology is, then, a dependent factor, dependent upon other long-term trends of change in a society. Both of these perspectives are illustrated nicely by the experience with birth control technology; where deep-seated values and interests inherent to rural life do not favor use of birth control devices, the existence of the devices per se does not call forth the required changes in values and interests. Where opposite conditions exist, for instance, in the United States, birth control technology and abortion have profound facilitating consequences for trends in the birth rate.[34]

Third, the full consequences of new technologies, in short, their "impact," awaits the transformation of society and organizational life, which in turn depends upon fundamentally nontechnological factors. The growth of public government use of computers in the last decade, which no doubt benefited computer firms, associated experts, and by extension, members of the academic and scientific establishment, was ultimately defeated by a number of governmental groups unwilling to make the transition to a managerial democracy.

These perspectives suggest a cautious strategy in the discussion of citizen technology. If, as we suggest, the various citizen technologies require for their use a transformation of democracy along this line or that, the question is, do we accept the consequences of that change? Even if a suitable technology and design which might facilitate the further development of democracy in the United States could be found, the question remains whether, given the nature of our society, powerful and organized groups would tolerate such a development or perhaps subvert the technology to serve their ends, which may not include democracy as a desideratum. On the other hand, while the development of citizen technology entails these risks, failure to develop a technological advantage for citizens may forever condemn them to the paternalism of expertise inherent in managerial democracy.

With these cautions in mind, let us look at the contemporary experiments and designs for citizen technology.

NOTES

1. Ithiel de Sola Poole, "Citizen Feedback in Political Philosophy," in *Talking Back,* ed. Ithiel de Sola Poole (Cambridge: MIT Press, 1973), p. 242.

2. For a long list of potential applications from solving the problems of world order to urban crime, see "Social Control Through Communications," by Dennis Gabor in *Communication Technology and Social Policy*, ed. George Gerbner, Larry Gross, William Melody (New York: Jonn Wiley, 1973).

3. Ithiel de Sola Poole, "The Rise of Communications Policy Research," *Journal of Communications* (Spring 1974): 32.

4. For a detailed study of decline in citizen donfidence and growth of alienation in public and private institutions in a local community, see Otis D. Duncan et al., *Social Change in a Metropolitan Community*, (New York: Russell Sage, 1973). For national trends, the Louis Harris index of alienation has increased from 29 percent of the population

alienated in 1966 to 55 percent in 1973. See the Harris Survey, New York *Post*, December 6, 1973. For national trends of decline of confidence in institutional leaders of both public and private sectors, see the General Social Surveys, 1973-75, of the National Opinion Research Corporation.

5. From a description of a panel discussion written by Martin Karnaugh for the International Conference on Communications, Philadelphia, June 1976, sponsored by the Institute of Electrical and Electronic Engineers.

6. Jay W. Forrester, *Urban Dynamics* (Cambridge: MIT Press, 1969). For similar proposals that do not rely on "systems analysis," see Edward C. Banfield, *The Unheavenly City Revisited* (Boston: Little, Brown, 1972).

7. For an account of computer use in American government, see Alan F. Westin with Michael Baker, *Databanks in a Free Society* (New York: Quadrangle Books, 1972), Chapter 2. See also James Martin and Adrian Norma, *The Computerized Society* (New York: Prentice Hall, 1972), Chapter 1.

8. Dieter Kimbel, "An Assessment of the Computerized Telecommunications Complex in Europe, Japan, and North America," in Gerbner et al., op. cit., Chapter 11.

9. Edwin B. Parker, with the assistance of Mark Porat, "Social Implications of Computer/Telecommunications Systems," *Program in Information Technology and Telecommunications*, Report No. 16 (Stanford: Center for Interdisciplinary Research, Stanford University, 1975).

10. Fritz Machlup, *The Production and Distribution of Knowledge in the United States* (Princeton: Princeton University Press, 1962).

11. "Computer Switching of Telephone Calls Put in Operation by A.T.T.," New York *Times*, January 18, 1976.

12. John E. Ward, "Present and Probably CATV/Broadband Communication Technology," in Poole, *Talking Back*, Chapter 9. There are much faster cable systems in commercial use specially designed for data transmission which operate at 500,000 hps. See Ephraim Kahn, "Commercial Uses of Broadband Communications," in Poole, *Talking Back*, Chapter 14.

13. Kahn, op. cit., p. 250.

14. George R. White, "Graphics Systems," in Gerbner et al., op cit., Chapter 5.

15. Poole, "The Rise of Communications Policy Research," p. 32.

16. Martin H. Seiden, *Cable Television U.S.A.* (New York: Praeger, 1972), p. 40.

17. Seiden, op. cit., Chapters 1 and 2.

18. Ralph Lee Smith, "CATV: FCC Rules and the Public Interest," in Gerbner et al., op. cit., Chapter 9; Richard Gabel, "Telecommunications Inter-Connection: Wherefrom and Whitherto?" in Gerbner et al., op. cit., Chapter 8.

19. William H. Melody, "The Role of Advocacy in Public Policy Planning," in Gerbner et al., op. cit., Chapter 12.

20. "House Unit Scores F.C.C. on Cable TV" New York *Times*, January 27, 1976.

21. "F.C.C. Rules on Cable TV Challenged" New York *Times*, February 6, 1976.

22. Nathan Katzman, "The Impact of Communication Technology: Promises and Prospects," *Journal of Communications*, Autumn 1974.

23. Daniel Bell, "The End of Ideology in the West," in Daniel Bell, *The End of Ideology* (New York: Free Press, 1960).

24. Bell, op. cit., p. 13.

25. Zbigniew Brzezinski, "The American Transition" *New Republic*, December 23, 1967; Daniel Bell, *The Coming of Post-Industrial Society* (New York: Basic Books, 1973), p. 14; and John Kenneth Galbraith, *The New Industrial State* (Boston: Houghton Mifflin, 1967), p. 73.

26. Bell, op. cit., p. 363.

27. Galbraith, op. cit., p. 380.

28. Brzezinski, op. cit., p. 20.

29. Brzezinski, ibid., p. 19.

30. A close reading of the later Marx shows how much he was fascinated, perhaps even taken in, by the new machines. Man would be displaced from labor, Marx argued, for instance, because machines would be produced to produce machines which would do the actual work. Man would cease even to be a "tool maker" by nature. See Karl Marx, *Capital* (New York: Modern Library, 1958), p. 406.

31. See the article on New Haven in "A City Where Computers Will Know About Everybody," *U.S. News and World Report*, May 15, 1967, p. 70.

32. See Kenneth Laudon, "Efficiency Versus Equity and Justice: Consequences of Public Sector Information Systems" (Paper presented at the Association of Computing Machinery Annual Meetings, Minneapolis, 1975). For an extended treatment see Kenneth Laudon, *Computers and Bureaucratic Reform* (New York: John Wiley, 1974). For specific references on the limitations of computers as actually used, see "Nadjari Stopped on Computer Plan," New York *Times*, February 17, 1975; and "H.E.W. Moves to Spur States to Seek Out Deserting Fathers," New York *Times*, March 5, 1975.

33. "Experts Rush to Create Unified City Accounting," New York *Times*, February 4, 1976.

34. George Daniels, "The Big Questions in the History of American Technology," *Technology and Culture* 11, no. 1 (1970).

2

CITIZEN TECHNOLOGY:
CONTEMPORARY DESIGNS
AND EXPERIMENTS

The worth of a State, in the long run, is the worth of the individuals composing it; and a State which postpones the interests of *their* mental expansion and elevation, to a little more of administrative skill, or of that semblance of it which practice gives, in details of business; a State which dwarfs its men in order that they may be more docile instruments in its hands, even for beneficial purposes, will find that with small men no really great thing can really be accomplished; and that the perfection of machinery to which it has sacrificed everything, will in the end avail it nothing, for want of the vital power which, in order that the machine might work more smoothly, it has preferred to banish.

J.S. Mill, "On Liberty"

The common ground on which various plans for citizen technology meet begins with a paradoxical feature of modern democracies like the United States: apathy, cynicism, and political withdrawal increase as literacy and access to education become more widespread. This is counter to the expectations of eighteenth and nineteenth century thinkers such as John Stuart Mill, as well as most modern-day liberals, who believed modern democracies are secure only through education and a broad distribution of the tools, techniques, and experience requisite to self-governance. The analysis of this paradox follows two interrelated paths. On the one hand, the growth of institutions into huge public and private leviathans effectively prevents ordinary persons from participating in decisions affecting their lives. Size per se dilutes the capacity of individuals and small groups to affect almost anything of importance in the modern organizational world.

The problem of the organizational gargantua is compounded in the twentieth century by peculiar developments of information technology. Either in the form of superabundant managerial technology, like computers, or in the more common form of propagative mass media which present the modern-day Pericles with unlimited audiences, the average adult has found himself increasingly the object of messages and commands originating from distant places and small groups fortunate enough to have access to and control over mass media.

The existence of media which require very large audiences who read, listen, and see, but who cannot on equal terms write, speak, and act (even if they have the mental ability to do so) suggests another paradox: while mass media have helped reduce traditional barriers to political participation such as literacy, education, and widespread dissemination of political information, it has not, at the same time, contributed new structured opportunities for participation. The result is a heightening sense of relative alienation: never before have so many been informed and aware of political issues, yet so relatively constrained by the nineteenth century institutions and techniques of political participation which characterize U.S. political life. Instead of providing the average person with new tools and techniques of influence over surrounding institutions commensurate with that person's heightened abilities, modern information technology comes to serve those very institutions as social control instruments which disseminate proper modes of etiquette, dress, demeanor, and speech.

A further consequence of the growth of peak organizations and modern information technology is the weakening of public policy itself.

Citizens more educated and informed than ever before in history feel less capable of influencing decisions of elected officials. Officials better advised and educated than their predecessors still find themselves unable to galvanize public opinion in support of their policies. Commenting on the continuing fall in voter turnout from 63 percent in 1960 to 55 percent in 1972, the political scientist Walter Burnham describes the result as a shredding away of political power:

> I don't see the basis for any positive majority on anything today. It creates a problem for any president in governing because in an atmosphere like this his power resources are likely to be shredded away whenever he takes a stand on anything of major importance.[1]

The withdrawal of legitimacy from existing political institutions, coupled with the failure to develop new forums of political participation, leads to the continual search for charismatic leaders and lengthy discussions in the public media over whether this or that politician has it. "Is he charismatic?" seems to be one of the more important questions asked of newly arrived officials.

The fundamental issue raised, then, is whether citizens can guide the development of society along lines that reflect their values and preferences or, as has been increasingly the case in the last several decades, they must adapt to the needs of ever-larger power blocs. Insofar as the former becomes impossible for want of appropriate political machinery, the escape is to look for charismatic leaders. And for lack of these in politics, citizens' resignation from political life follows.

MASS-PARTICIPATION TECHNOLOGY

These are the threads that bind the various plans for citizen technology. Together they are attempts to overcome the effects of huge organizational size by providing the average citizen with new tools of political influence. Moreover, if the cost in time and money of using these tools of influence is sufficiently low, then it is hoped a new participatory democracy will follow. The question that remains is how might this be done and with what consequences.

The most common answer is to strengthen the direct linkage between citizens and leaders through the use of mass participation technologies. There are three different varieties of mass participation plans:

Opinion-Polling Devices for Policy Formation

Advances in the accuracy of sampling methods have led to increasing respectability of opinion polls. However, the technology exists, or nearly exists, to do away with sampling and to attempt to read electronically the opinions of the population universe under study. The National Public Affairs Television Network, a division of the Public Broadcasting Service (PBS), sponsored for two years a debate program, "The Advocates," in which experts, a studio audience, and debaters posed issues to the listening audiences. During and after the program listeners would call in their support or opposition to some policy; during the program and in the following week's program, the results of viewer opinion were shown. Similarly, the Regional Plan Association in New York supported a program called "Choices for '76" in which television viewers in the metropolitan region viewed films on public policy options, and subsequently mailed ballots indicating their choice of policy option in to the program.[2]

These programs rely upon a rather primitive "call-in" technology; with the change of the telephone system to computer switching circuits a more sophisticated "sweep-out" technology is close at hand.

One such "sweep-out" technology plan calls for a monthly national plebiscite on federal government decisions. Described by its originators, Clark McCauley, James Rood, and Paul Johnson (a social psychologist, an engineer, and a physicist respectively) the national plebiscite would work in four phases.[3] Using a federal national television network, the government would "prime" the process for one month by presenting an issue (such as a national gas tax) and giving its policy by testimony from the various government agencies involved.

Second, experts from within and without the government would give their views during the same month. The month of government proposal and expert discussion would culminate with a debate among interested and affected parties. Finally, at the end of the month, the citizen would plug a "voting terminal" into his telephone; a regional computer would verify the authenticity of the connection; and the citizen would vote on one of the policy options by punching a series of numbers into the voting terminal. The regional computer would read the vote by sweeping the phone circuits of all plugged-in citizens. The results would appear a few minutes later on the national television network; a few minutes after that, the same procedure would be used to choose the next month's issue.

To assure articulation with the real decision-making process, results of the plebiscite would have to be voted on within a month and would become law if passed by Congress. The plebiscite would function then "as a committee of Congress, a 'committee of the whole' able to bring legislation in the national interest before the Congress." Although not stated in the proposal, presumably the traditional checks on congressional power would exist: legislation could be vetoed by the president or struck down by the courts.

A somewhat less ambitious but presumably more feasible design in the near future is the mass-participation feedback system designed by E.J. Corwin, which is being advertised under the registered service mark of "CITIZENS RESPONSE" ®.[4] This is a semiautomated polling system that operates as follows: the government (local, state, or national) informs citizens that it is interested in their opinion on some issue, and mails them specially designed IBM cards on which citizens are asked to indicate their degree of support or opposition to a specific program. In addition, citizens are asked to indicate their position on several demographic measures such as income, race, sex, age, and so forth. The results are mailed into a regional or central computer-processing facility where, by virtue of the specially designed cards, the computer can read and verify citizen opinions immediately without additional keypunching or human intervention. Results of polls can become available within 24 hours and can be posted in public locations or broadcast over local outlets.

Rather than a simple one-shot static poll, the efficiency of the system should permit a moving poll in which citizens would be asked for responses on the same issue a week or perhaps a month later. The system allows citizens to change their positions after governmental leaders or other groups attempt to mobilize citizen opinions along desired lines.

In most respects the Corwin system is like the Regional Plan Association "Choices for '76" program and others like it (Dallas' "Goals for Dallas"), with the exception that these other programs used traditional questionnaires which required keypunching, and were attempted only once. The point of the Corwin system is its greater efficiency of input forms and the notion of continuous feedback in which citizens are permitted to change their opinions over a period of time, and to perceive some sort of dynamic image of changing public opinion.

The precise relationship of the polls' results to political decisions is left unclear in the published designs. Funding for the design would apparently be aided by commercial use of some of the information (especially demographic profiles); administration of polls could eventually be handled by the postal service. The Corwin plan seeks to account for the possiblity of unrepresentative responses by suggesting that opinion results of various demographic groups could be weighted and extrapolated to the entire nation. The system has been used with college students, the Los Angeles PBS viewing area on "The Advocates" show, and in the Fifth Planning District of Virginia. Corwin hopes to use the system to cover the entire state of Virginia in 1976.

From a critical perspective, these plans, which are based on some kind of opinion polling, suffer from a common defect: each seeks to strengthen the vertical communication linkages between societal decision makers and citizens. While at first glance this seems desirable, several harmful consequences are possible. The emphasis on vertical linkages means not only that citizens will presumably have a greater control over decision makers, but also that decision makers and politicians and other elites will have greater access to citizens. The priming devices upon which these mass systems rely are usually government-controlled channels; the participants in the priming events necessarily will be a handful of recognized elites, for example, academic, business, labor, and so forth. In this sense these opinion-polling plans only strengthen the already large broadcast opportunities of elite groups in the society.

The opinion-polling devices are "atomizing" in both their assumptions and perhaps effects as well. The basic notion of each is that individual citizens will confront and decide the issues of the day in their isolated homes in front of some broadcast device. Yet this assumption is highly atomistic and contrary to most research, which shows that political opinions are formed in the context of community subgroups of which citizens are members, for example, work groups, churches, neighborhoods, as well as formal voluntary associations.

Worse yet is the potential of these devices for actually causing a further atomization of society. If the locus of political attitude formation shifts from subgroup settings to the isolation booths of millions of homes, the protective functions of subgroups will be lost. Bereft of the advice, political savvy, and information provided by peers in group settings, the citizen becomes more "mobilizable," more accessible, than at present. Weakening these subgroups by providing functional political alternatives to their existence removes an important structural check on the power of societal elites.

The opinion-polling plans fail to enhance, and perhaps weaken, existing horizontal communication and influence linkages in the society. Communication among citizens and small groups tends to be forgotten in the attempt to strengthen the citizen-elite linkages. Presumably these plans would be able to greatly enhance the role of the citizen in shaping public policy. But even here questions arise. In the Corwin plan, based on the mailing of opinion cards, there appears to be no direct linkage between citizen opinions and resulting policy decisions. What happens if opinion opposes a certain decision? The answer appears to be that politicians will use the broadcast channels to change opinion along lines dictated by "national interests":

> True leadership will not have to submit to the dictate of the polls. On the contrary. Thru an on-going dialogue with citizens it will be able to measure the initial attitudes of support or rejection, and inform citizens more fully why the unpopular course of action is recommended. In turn the reaction to this second phase of com- municiation can measure the effectiveness of new disclosures and arguments. This ongoing exchange of ideas must continue until citizens realize the reasons and voice their support, which in a democracy is an indispensable condition of a successful and lasting progress.[5]

In short, unacceptable feedback of the citizens will be changed by the very system that is supposed to reflect their desires!

In the McCauley et al. proposal, which relies on computer sweeping of home voting machines, the connection to societal decision making is more traditional: the results of the poll will be treated as a "committee of the whole" report, which must be voted on by Congress in 30 days. This strong articulation to decision making no doubt will increase the citizen's interest in the system, but one wonders if it is not too strong. Complex issues, like energy conservation and tax reform, may require more time than one month to discuss and decide. Moreover, one wonders how a congressman will react to the voting poll. If the national opinion is contrary to constituent opinion, how should he vote? Obviously he will seek to remain in office and ignore the national polling results. If the Congress ignores the poll, what can the public do? What forces can the public marshal to its cause?

Indeed, the most interesting question raised by the McCauley plan is, What can the public do if the entire Congress ignores the results of the poll, or votes contrary to the poll? No doubt the citizenry can become outraged at the poor taste of congressmen who insult the national will; no doubt congress- men who do so will find good public reasons for ignoring the collective will. But legislation does not get passed simply becuase of public opinion support for this or that piece of legislation. If this were the case, the United States would have had federal aid to education in 1958 (instead of 1964) and a medical insurance plan by 1960 (which has not yet passed Congress).[6] Instead legislation is passed (or stalled) through the organized efforts of vitally affected interest groups, which may or may not represent public opinion.

If legislation is considered an outcome of organized lobbying efforts by various societal subgroups, then it can be seen that the opinion-polling techniques represent no great advantage for the citizenry. Indeed, the technology outlined in these plans will not increase one whit the political and organizational skills of citizens in translating public opinion into legislation. The hidden assumption in these mass-opinion plans is that if congressmen fail to heed the public will, the citizens will rise up and throw them out of office. But this requires organization within local constituencies and within state political machines. How will the technology improve the ability of citizens and local groups to organize locally? The answer is simply that it will not. Hence congressmen would have little to fear by ignoring the national voting poll, or tabling the committee of the whole recommendations for further study. The citizenry may become outraged but certainly will remain largely incapable of acting.

Taken at their strongest point as attempts to establish a direct vertical link between citizen and decision maker, and forgetting momentarily the undesirability of such a link, these opinion plans seeking a "collective will" raise serious questions. At the very least we should expect of new citizen technologies that they increase, in the words of Mill, the citizens' administrative and organizational skills. Necessarily this implies that horizontal linkages between citizens and local groups would have to be strengthened first to encourage local dialogues and coalitions (a congressman is much more impressed by large, organized local groups than he is by opinion polls of his district). Only in such a manner will citizens develop sufficient power to affect materially societal decisions.

Automated and Semiautomated Feedback Programs

A second somewhat different kind of mass-participation citizen technology seeks to improve the political decision makers' sense of how well existing policies are working. Generally these plans seek less the participation of individuals in the actual formulation of policy, than they do an efficient way for administrators to hear from the citizens and, vice versa, to provide new ways for the average citizen to talk back.

In the 1960s there occurred in local governments of the United States a veritable explosion of efforts to increase the responsiveness of government to complaints of citizens. Whether in the form of New York City's Urban Action Task Force, Little City Halls of Boston, or Puerto Rico's Citizen Feedback System, they represent the elected officials' response to increasingly vocal complaints that the bureaucracy of government ignores citizens. In part this is a structural feature built into the society: 80 to 90 percent of the decisions made by government are made in bureaucracies and never see the light of political day, let alone debate.[7] By and large, these so-called administrative decisions are made without hearings, due process, or the normal protections afforded citizens whenever their interests are being decided. Therefore it seems sensible to inquire how technology might enlarge the nature of these decisions to include broader interests.

Most of the program developed in the 1960s relied upon very simple technologies, primarily the telephone, and the creation of single numbers or groups of numbers where citizens could phone complaints, suggestions, and responses to current administrative practices. Most of these programs, as it turns out, seek to provide a governmental response to a specific citizen complaint. Typical is the New York City Mayor's Action Center begun under the Lindsay administration and carried on by the Beame administration. As a part of other efforts (such as decentralized city halls and urban action task forces) the Mayor's Action Center was established to take citizen complaints by mayoral aides (volunteers and paid staff), direct them to the appropriate agency, and in some cases develop an immediate response. The citizen receives a letter shortly thereafter explaining what action the mayor's office took.

Unfortunately many of these feedback programs do little more than respond to brush fires. Thus the Mayor's Action Center may be effective in insuring delivery of hot water in a single slum tenement but be quite incapable of changing the administrative and political policies that led to the problem in the first place.

A more sophisticated higher-technology project which goes considerably beyond simple feedback systems is the Feedback-Dialog System of John D.C. Little and others of the Operations Research Center of Massachusetts Institute of Technology (MIT).[8] Operating out of the Governor's Office of Public Service, the MIT project developed an interactive computer program to allow for categorization, storage, and subsequent retrieval by interested parties of citizen complaint cases. The addition of secondary computer processing to citizen complaints allows the complaints to be analyzed monthly in terms of location of complaint, type, agency involved, names of aides responsible for answering the case, and so forth. In short, citizen complaints could be used as indicators of general problem areas, faulty programs, and failures of administration. The system was designed to permit others besides the governor, such as the legislature, organized community groups, and other citizens to have access to the data. Unfortunately the research program ended before any of these aims were accomplished.

Yet the most interesting aspect of the MIT project was the attempt to build so-called feedforward links from government to citizen with the assistance of technological aids. Feedforward, in English, means confronting citizens with various policy options and allowing them to dialogue about the value assumptions of these policies, suggest new options, and in some cases test out the consequences of choosing various options.

One feedforward project involved the use of "listening posts": 12 citizen group meetings in towns and villages of Massachusetts. Arranged with the help of the League of Women Voters and the State Department of Education, the local groups discusses the current goals of secondary education, how they are perceived, and what they should be. Each of the listening posts employed a portable audience feedback device. Each member of the audience was given a box with six response categories connected to a publicly visible register which displayed the selections of participants. The system had a capacity of 512 participants. At appropriate moments in the dialogue among citizens a moderator would ask participants to indicate their degree of support for the various options. The device seemed to be a stimulus to additional participation, and the organization of meetings allowed citizens to put their own proposals up for a group vote. On the other hand, the small number of participants at any one meeting (usually 20 to 40) probably meant the technology was of no particular advantage when compared to hand votes except that the electronic voting was anonymous and might have allowed persons with unpopular views to express then.

A second aspect of the feedforward project involved the use of computerized models of complex policy decisions by interested citizen groups. Operations researchers developed models based on real data of two forthcoming policy decisions: higher education tuition and secondary school financing. Based on historical data, a time-sharing computer could be queried by remote terminal to point out the consequences of choosing various policy options.

The interesting aspect of this innovation is, of course, that it illustrates how citizen groups might be given access to the same kinds of advanced policy-formation tools heretofore reserved for elites. Potentially, through remote terminals in community areas, "a variety of people and groups could have access to a computer analysis, could put in their own assumptions and proposed actions, and could evaluate the results for themselves." In the case of the Local School Financing Model, various opposing groups from the Educational Conference Board, Advisory Council on Education, the Department of Education, to the governor's office and legal groups developing court briefs, used the system with the assistance of the researchers to develop their proposals for alternatives to property tax school financing.

From a critical perspective it is clear that many aspects of the MIT project are beyond the technological reach of the society in the immediate future. The day is far off when citizens will be able to walk into a community center and test their assumptions against a computer reality model, although television call-in programs might be utilized not to broaden public access to computer-assisted policy models.

Several impressive features of the MIT project stand out, however. First, the technologies were developed in the context of existing agencies and decision routines, which gives them a quality of realism often missing in other research. The technologies, instead of overwhelming the traditional systems of administration and policy making, tended to act as "add-on" devices. Rather than assuming or encouraging an atomized citizenry, the feedforward programs worked with existing community subgroups and interest groups.

Unlike other feedback programs, this research recognizes the distinction between feedback and participation, albeit in the form of feedforward. One of the things we might expect from a citizen technology is that it enhance the reasoning power and organizational skills of average citizens. Participation is more than somehow "including the preferences of citizens in policy decisions"; ultimately it must include the notion of citizens rationally discussing policy options among themselves and organizing to ensure their adoption.

Yet unfortuantely in none of these plans is the distinction between participation and feedback drawn clearly enough. Too often—as with opinion polling—participation reduces to feedback which further reduces to large-scale psychotherapy designed to reduce the "psychological sense of alienation" and to provide moral uplift without actually providing any additional net influence to the average person. One engineer's rhapsodic description of feedback programs illustrates how easily this can happen:

> These examples point up one very important aspect of such citizen feedback or response aggregation systems: that is, that they can *educate and involve* the participants without the necessity that the responses formally determine a decision. Indeed, the teaching-learning function may be the most important.[9]

The flip side of the citizen participation coin in regard to these plans is the expert paternalism typical of managerial democracy. It would seem the latter has as much probability of appearing as the former, should these systems ever be made operational.

Media to the Masses

The third variety of citizen technology seeks to provide average citizens with direct access to the tools of mass communication. Based largely upon the development in the late 1960s of hand-held television cameras, which required little skill to operate, and videotape machines that provided mobility to television cameras, these plans are established on the notion that conventional mass media operate to prevent people from taking control of their lives. Redistribute this prop of the status quo by opening the studios up to "the people" who could tell their story, and the powerless will become powerful:

> Power is no longer measured in land, labor, or capital, but by access to information and the means to disseminate it. As lcng as the most powerful tools (not weapons) are in the hands of those who would hoard them, no alternative cultural vision can succeed. Unless we design and implement alternate information structures which transcend and reconfigure the existing ones, other alternate systems and life styles will be no more than products of the existing process.
>
> Television is not merely a better way to transmit the old culture, but an element in the foundation of a new one.
>
> Our species will survive neither by totally rejecting nor unconditionally embracing technology—but by humanizing it: by allowing people access to the information tools they need to shape and reassert control over their lives.[10]

Ordinarily we might dismiss such prophecy as simplistic, were it not for the fact that the idea of literally giving the media to "the people" came to play an important role in the FCC regulation of the cable industry in the early 1970s.

Rarely avoiding an opportunity to place cable television at a competitive disadvantage with regular broadcast television, the 1972 FCC ruling declared that all cable systems with more than 3,500 subscribers, and systems in the top 100 markets, would have to provide by 1977 up to 4 public-access channels and facilities which the public could use to broadcast original programs.[11]

Theoreticians of public access cable television, like Theodora Sklover of Public Access in New York, point to the "engineered messages of 'real life,' edited to the bone, paced for action, promulgated by 3 of 4 sources—the major networks" as the villains which prevent the public from "experiencing the media actively, not passively." Others see public-access TV as "the ideal vehicle of communication for a truly pluralistic, participatory society, and the revivial of local activism and community spirit."[12]

The two cable systems that have the longest experience with public access are Sterling Cable Television's Open Channel in Manhattan and Station Theta in Los Angeles. Since operations began in 1970, an impressive array of groups has used the Manhattan public-access channels, ranging from the Museum of Modern Art, the Psycho Education Department of Coney Island Hospital, the Society for Creative Anachronism, to the American Arbitration Association. Programming hours have tripled from 2,000 in 1972 to over 6,000 in 1975. The vast majority of the programs involve community information, entertainment, and religious programs. In the words of one supporter, the "New York experience shows growth toward grassroots programming not available on other channels."[13]

The production data look impressive until one asks about who is watching at the other end. As it turns out, the public-access production staff often outnumbers the listening audience. the net result, in the words of one critic, is that public-access TV channels "are providing access by the public but not to the public."[14]

One study of a 3,500-subscriber cable system in Columbus, Indiana, "The Athens of the Prairie," found that even in this relatively large cable system, only 20 people (3 percent) had watched anything on public access in a week. This is about 0.2 percent of all television viewing for the week. Rudy Bretz, a Rand Corporation specialist in communication, estimates that during peak viewing hours when about 65 percent of the sets are tuned in, at most, nine or ten sets would be tuned to public access. With two viewers per set that means 18 or 20 persons are "participating."[15]

Using these estimates as a guide to the much larger city systems, such as New York's Sterling Cable Television (29,000 subscribers) and Teleprompter Cable Television (40,000), a prime-time audience for public access might range from 75 to 104 viewers. This is in a city of 8 million residents!

The cost of operating Sterling Cable Television's public-access channels for one year, 1974, was $80,000, including investment in Sony Portapaks, cameras, and production facilities. This has led some to think that public-access channels are cheap.[16] But with an average subscriber cost of $14, gross revenues are only slightly over $450,000. The public channels represent about 18 percent of gross revenues. This is to benefit prime-time Sterling Cable audiences of 75 persons.

However, let's play with the cable fable. Let us assume Congress is capable of taking the FCC wraps off cable, and further assume enough money was invested to "wire up" New York City's approximately 3 million television households on a single cable system. What kind of public-access audience would appear? Using the above estimates, in a totally wired New York, about 3,900 households with 7,800 viewers could be expected at the peak hour, 8:30 p.m.

This is more impressive, but even under these fantastic assumptions the result is hardly the stuff from which "alternative cultural visions" will flow.

Moreover, if things got better, they could actually become worse. Several studies of public-access television show that the most successful groups who use the channels are those that do a good deal of prior organization to inform their members and the larger public through newspaper, radio, and other spot announcements. If public-access television ever were to draw a large audience, groups like the existing local Democratic club, General Motors Acceptance Corporation, and Labor Councils would begin competing for an audience with the less well-organized Veterans Against the War, the local Yoga club, and the Good Citizens League. Few doubt who would win such a competition and there is no elegant way for determining which group should have access, at what time.

Moreover, even if a much larger viewing audience would habitually appear during prime time in search of what the National Broadcasting Company (NBC) calls the LOP (least objectionable program), the problem of allocating access to this now valuable resource is rarely mentioned by theoreticians of public-access television. There is a limited prime time: from 6 to 10 p.m., one-half of the sets are in use, whereas from 6 a.m. to 3 p.m., use ranges from 10 to 15 percent.[17] There is a limited number of channels. If more public-access channels are opened up, the audience becomes splintered into that many different programs, and the value of the technology for reaching large numbers of homes declines. If public-access channels are limited to a few, each with a reasonably large audience, many groups will compete for the resource. This, in turn, diminishes the chance for any single group to influence public opinion.

One potential way around these limitations is the suggestion that the cable companies be forced to operate on a neighborhood basis. Indeed, Sterling Cable Television must by 1977 develop a capacity to allow for local program origination in ten separate neighborhoods it serves. Programs will originate in neighborhoods, and reception would be similarly restricted. Yet one wonders if the same limitations described above would simply reappear on this new level. One wonders if the reduction in scale of operation would not also decrease viewer interest and "participation." Most of what we now know suggests that when organized in this fashion, public access will forever be condemned to providing access by a few people to the tools of television production, rather than to an audience.

CRITICAL SUMMARY OF
MASS-PARTICIPATION TECHNOLOGY

The experiments and plans for electronic mass participation raise three related issues. The first concerns the problem of size. Each of the plans described above hopes to overcome the fact that the voice of individual citizens and their organized groups is overwhelmed in large nations with populations of 200 million, and in large private and public organizations where they work. The key words here are *participation, feedback,* and *sense of alienation.* Yet, as we have seen, the mass-participation experiments solve the problem of influence only by distorting the meaning of *participation,* which ordinarily implies an active involvement in the formation and implementation of public policy. Even friendly critics of the mass-participation plans like Ithiel de Sola Poole, in his endorsement of automated complaint centers which send out computer letters to complaining citizens, end up in this dilemma:

> Modern society needs better modes of communication between the people and those in power. It needs to lessen the citizen's sense of alienation, his sense of powerlessness and isolation. . . . Better communication technologies that create more efficient, more extensive and more intensive interaction between public figures and their constituents may reduce the sense of alienation by making the public figures better able to *respond* to their constituents and to *influence* them. There is no electronic difference between these two processes. They are both enhanced by efficient two-way conversation.[18]

Plans that begin lamenting the lack of participation opportunities end up proposing to reduce the citizen's sense of alienation. Hence, the problem of size is solved by redefining the nature of the democratic process itself. Instead of an organization of power that permits groups of citizens to shape public policy, political democracy becomes instead a mechanism to reduce the psychic pain caused in part by the problem of size.

Even here it is dubious to argue that filling out a questionnaire, punching a button on the home voting box, or calling in a response to the local television station where "experts" analyze the aggregate opinion, will in any way reduce even the sense of alienation and powerlessness. Rather, these devices may stand out as additional symbols of the lowly state to which the citizen is reduced. We must ask if the political system is really very good as psychotherapy, and if perhaps other institutions might not be better suited to deliver such services.

A second issue raised by these plans is the general problem of time. One of the virtues of democracy as it stands at present is that the formulation of domestic public policy usually requires a long time—on the order of several years for most major pieces of legislation in health, education, and welfare. While often painfully slow, this extended period allows a hearing to affected groups, consideration of alternative policies, and full deliberation of issues.

If plans for mass participation were taken seriously, that is, if the results of the feedback were strongly articulated with decision making in executive or legislative processes, these virtues of democracy would be lost. Recognizing this, many of the designers of such systems advocate a weak articulation with the real decision-making process. The result of this limitation is the transformation of citizen technology into just another mental health program. There is no compelling reason to alter democracy by racing the decision process simply because a technology has arrived that can do this.

A related dimension of the time issue involves the question of who would participate. The presumption is that reducing the personal cost in time and effort of political participation will result in large numbers of citizens using the new mass technologies. But this is contrary to much of what is known about political participation. Only about 5 percent of the electorate are ever actively involved in political campaigns, and then only in peak periods of interest such as presidential elections.[19] Most of the plans above involve the average person listening to some priming event like a group of experts or leaders, which is followed by a vote. But public affairs programming is watched by only about 3 percent of the available audience, and the remaining 97 percent watch entertainment shows.* There is no reason to believe this pattern will change because of a monthly national television referendum, the importance of which for actual decision making is dubious. Moreover, if the mass-participation plans were implemented, and even if they attracted 3 percent of the audience monthly, how representative is the audience of the electorate? Corwin above suggests weighting of the viewers to compensate for the likely fact that viewers in the Northeast and Midwest would watch more than viewers in the West and South. Yet who would believe such weighting (were it possible) and who would wish important decisions of the Republic to depend on this cooking of the data?

As it turns out, politics in the sense of debates among various points of view is boring for the average citizen. After eight hours of work, average Americans watch television about four hours a day, largely to escape reality, not to immerse themselves in more of it.[20] Political participation is highly interest-

---

*In some special cases, like the "Adams Chronicles" shown in 1976 over WNET-TV in New York, the educational television audience will bulge to 15 percent. Generally, however, even in New York, audience ratings rarely exceed 3 percent and have remained at that level for several years. See the New York *Times*, February 4, 1976.

graded: people who are interested in politics seek out information and knowledge commensurate with their interest.

The vision that participation will involve rolling off the couch and pushing a voting button and thereby result in a politically meaningful national response, fails to recognize that most citizens just don't care that much about politics. If the electronic polls were limited to educational and moral uplift functions, the level of interest generated would at best produce the 3 percent of the audience that now watches educational television.

Related to this aspect of the time problem is yet another: all cannot talk to all. This limitation is especially crucial for those plans promising access to the media. The number of possible communication links between persons in a group grows exponentially with the size of the group. A committee of six active persons can discuss an issue and plan some action in two hours; a similar group of ten can discuss an issue in two hours; in a group of 30 active members it may take several hours for everyone to air their views, with additional time to plan some action. Any citizen technology which hopes to allow citizens media access to express their views will run into the problem that if it works, and citizens start lining up at the studio, there will not be enough channels to go around, and, just as important, not enough time in the day for citizens to listen to all these views.

The third issue raised by the current plans for citizen technology is: who gains what? In terms of the distribution of benefits, we can see that the politicians and their hired experts, those who run the priming events, gain an additional access channel to public opinion which bypasses completely any intermediate institutions. The message goes directly to the home. Currently these direct messages are limited to occasional presidential addresses to the nation; with the plans above, they would become regular prime-time fare.

What does the average citizen gain? He gains a questionnaire to fill out, a voting box connected to his cable television, or in the case of public access, use of a television channel. What unites these benefits is that they are appurtenances not connected to anything of significance. Television channels which no one watches, and electronic tabulators to reduce the sense of alienation are the stuff of *1984*, not the tools of revitalizing tired democracies.

If we look to citizen technology in the hope of promoting interaction among grassroots groups, enhancing the ability of these groups to reach a consensus on political issues and to form coalitions in advance of their cause, then it is apparent that mass-participation technology is not the answer. The political risk of generating a mass society based on strong, direct electronic links between leaders and the led, and the social risk of further atomizing the society to the level of living-room democracy, are far greater than any likely benefits.

INTERACTIVE TECHNOLOGIES

If the "fit" between mass participation technology and democracy is not ideal, as we suggest it is not, another family of technologies may hold some promise. This family we have characterized loosely as interactive technology. As we have seen propagative mass-communication technologies are marvelously overdeveloped; amateurs can now carry cameras and hidden microphones almost everywhere, and instant computerized national plebescites are off the drawing boards and seeking a place to be used. Interactive technology, on the other hand, is severely underdeveloped.

Simply put, an interactive communication system is one in which the message of one person or a group can be responded to by other persons or groups immediately. Ordinary conversation, meetings of up to, say, 5,000 in a common hall, and much smaller committees are examples of technologically unaided interactive systems. An electronic technology which functions to support interactive systems we can call an interactive technology.

The crucial behavioral difference between interactive and mass-participation technology is simply that the former allows for mutual and direct influence among the users of the technology. Participation in a small seminar or a telephone conference call is thus inherently different from participating in a television program by viewing the same. In the words of a psychologist, "interactive participation is regenerative" and capable of restructuring the motivation of participants.[21]

The telephone is a simple electronic interactive technology usually limited to two people, although add-on devices like amplified two-way speakers can be used to allow widely separated small groups of persons to communicate. Farmers in Iowa meeting in National Farm Organization halls in different countries frequently use such add-on devices to discuss daily crop reports, planting schedules, and commodity prices.

A slightly more complex interactive system is the telephone conference call. Unlike the above example, in which two groups of farmers can communicate using a single telephone connection, in conference calls an operator connects up to 30 separate telephones into a single circuit somewhat like a very large party line. Much beyond 30, and the technical quality declines markedly. In the fully automated electronic telephone exchanges now being introduced, operator assistance is not required for up to four-person conference calls.

With these exceptions, there are no interactive electronic technologies currently available to the public. Two-way cable television is largely a dream, and even here the systems envisaged are not interactive like the telephone system which allows people to call one another on demand. Orlando, Florida, has the only commercial two-way cable system in the country that is used primarily to pretest television commercials. Each family rates commercials by punching keys on a home voting box; a computer then sweeps the network every few seconds to tally the ratings. Inasmuch as this system does not currently allow communication among the 500 families, it is not in any sense interactive, but instead is a prototype of the mass-participation technology outlined above. Unfortunately, the commercial worth of this type of two-way cable will most likely increase in the future and we can expect its eventual spread.

Computer technologists have developed the most advanced large-scale interactive systems which are used primarily for commercial, governmental, and scientific use. With the development of second- and third-generation computers in the early 1960s, it became possible to share the enormous memory capacity of large computers among thousands of users. Called "Time Sharing Systems" (TSS), these systems allow individuals at isolated terminals to interact with a set of data stored in a computer often thousands of miles away. Thousands of other users may be interacting with their separate data files simultaneously; the computer switches back and forth from one user to another so fast that the terminal operator perceives almost instantaneous response. Common-carrier airline reservation systems are time-sharing systems. In some TSS systems, such as those found in several state criminal justice information systems, isolated terminal operators can send messages to other terminals or all terminals at once through computerized message switching.[22] With these horizontal linkages some computer systems are fully interactive.

These applications of interactive communication systems are restricted to governmental, scientific, and certain high-load commercial applications. Yet the principal of their operation is potentially applicable to political processes as well. Unfortunately it is only in the distant future that even primitive facsimiles of these advanced systems could become available to ordinary citizens.

The traditional mass media (principally newspapers, radio, and television), however, have always sought to capture certain elements of interactive systems. Newspapers invite opposition editorials from the readership (for example, the New York *Times* Op-Ed page). Radio stations have call-in programs to let listeners speak to others. In the New York City area a very large experiment called the Metropolitan Regional Plan tried to combine television broadcasting with local discussion groups followed by a poll.[23] Voluntary organizations, labor groups, and local business groups were encouraged to view with their members the several public affairs programs broadcast on several local stations. In this way the plebiscitarian feature of ordinary public affairs programs broadcast to individual homes could be avoided.

These innovations tend either to miss the point or simply fail. Opening up the broadcast to let readers or listeners speak more often than not stimulates those with the most outrageous and deviant positions to call in. Moreover, an interaction does not take place: one person speaks, then another, then another, often with little growth in mutual understanding. As long as broadcasting is from one single point to millions in the audience, in essence little has changed and the opportunities for participation are severely limited.

In the case of the Metropolitan Regional Plan Association experiment, the innovation seems to have failed. Quite often local groups failed to organize their members to watch the programs; the organization of this mammoth experiment which was to involve over 2 million citizens (from broadcast to final polling) was confused.

More important perhaps in the case of the Regional Plan experiment, it was not possible for geographically disparate groups to talk with one another, or to form coalitions.

INTERGOVERNMENTAL EXPERIMENT: MRC-TV

One of the largest, ongoing experiments with interactive technology is Metropolitan Regional Council Television (MRC-TV), based in New York City. Its principal function is to provide an "on-demand" communications network for local governments in the New York metropolitan region.

Among the more important subgroups in U.S. society are the thousands of local governments that dot the landscape. In New York City alone there are 1,400 such local governments, from water and planning districts to borough governments; in the New York metropolitan region there are over 500 major municipal, city, county, intercounty, state, and interstate governments. To the extent that many urban problems cannot be solved by any one local government, cooperation and communication among these local governments (or the lack thereof) is an important determinant of the quality of life within urban regions.

Efforts to combine local governments and districts into single metropolitan governments, sponsored by the Ford Foundation and local progressive groups in the late 1950s, failed generally to capture popular support, except in a few areas such as Miami.[24] Suburban voters were hardly persuaded by the argument that they should help support social investments in the central cities upon which their livelihood often rested.

In any event, one of the more promising potentials in certain new computer and telecommunications technologies in the early 1960s was that the functional need for governmental reorganization of metropolitan regions could be lessened if information could be more efficiently transferred among local governments. One appeal of the very large third-generation computers emerging in the 1960s was precisely that administrative intelligence on people, places, and things could be transferred efficiently among autonomous local governments. The continued growth through the 1970s of integrated information systems linking together various functional agencies, for example, police and welfare, across city, county, and state lines is testimony to the fact that to some extent technological change has obviated the need for certain kinds of political reorganization in the United States.[25]

Yet other kinds of intergovernment functions were ignored by the new computer information systems. Local governments need to share planning information, they need frequently to coordinate political efforts to obtain funding from state and federal authorities, and they need to share experiences about successful and unsuccessful programs (for example, various options in waste disposal, transportation, education, and police areas).

One experiment designed to meet these other needs for intergovernmental communication and coordination is the Metropolitan Regional Council (New York) closed circuit television (MRC-TV).[26] The Metropolitan Regional Council is a voluntary association of New York metropolitan governments. The principal function of this group is to share information among local governments and to coordinate lobbying efforts in the states of New York, New Jersey, and Connecticut. MRC, with funding from the National Science Foundation and local governments and businesses, developed a closed circuit microwave television station located in the World Trade Center, New York City. The station connects 17 local government buildings in the region making possible broadcasting from the central station as well as point-to-point communication through the central station. For instance, Elizabeth, New Jersey, public officials could hold a teleconference with officials of Bridgeport, Connecticut. Alternatively, all 17 governments can receive a single broadcast on new federal solid waste regulations, for example, and follow this with a group discussion of local responses to the federal law.

In terms of utilization, the MRC-TV concept seems to have been accepted by the local governments involved. Programming of teleconferences has increased severalfold since 1973 to a current daily program of five hours. Uses other than teleconferencing are traditional broadcasts to all local governments of police, fire, and welfare agency training films and lectures.

THE CHINESE BOXES

Quite clearly, the MRC-TV experiment does not address itself to the problem of how local citizen groups can come to exert greater influence over local governments. But an interesting question is raised by the experiment. What if a citizen technology was developed that increased the influence of ordinary citizens over their local governments but failed to similarly increase the influence of local governments vis-a-vis state and federal governments? Given the great dependence of municipal and county government upon state and federal financing, and hence given the multilayer nature of democracy in the United States as it actually is, the prospect is that a narrowly defined citizen technology would allow citizens more influence over an empty shell called local government. We will return to this problem in subsequent chapters. Suffice it to say now that a realistic citizen technology would have to increase the influence of local level subgroups over larger entities as well as address the problem of how individual citizens relate to local subgroups.

CONCLUSION

Currently, the interactive technologies are not well developed, with perhaps the exception of operator-assisted conference telephone calls. It is inconceivable that in the near future closed circuit point-to-point microwave transmission of television will become widely used. Indeed, if it were, the available air space would be quickly used up. AT&T, after giving up on an investment of several hundred million dollars in a new gadget called "picture phone," has developed a five-station teleconferencing network connecting studies in New York, Philadelphia, New Jersey, Chicago, and Washington, D.C. While the average person is not willing to pay $50 a month for individual picture phones, large corporations are willing to lease the conference studios from AT&T. Even here, the expense of coming to the studios and high lease costs inhibit widespread commercial use.

Setting aside for the moment the difficulties that limit its availability, the virtue of interactive technology is that, unlike mass-participation and data-transformation technology, it permits the concurrent adjustment of differing views and mutual influence between speakers and listeners.

If we consider the currently available 30-person telephone conference call, it seems to fit the bare social requirements of political participation in a democracy: the promotion of interaction and adjustment of views, consensus building, and formation of coalitions and plans for political action. While the other technologies described above must reduce participation to the level of punching a button or filling out questionnaires in response to some centrally generated program, the interactive technologies require no "head-end," or central studio. In this sense, the interactive technologies strengthen the potential for horizontal communication among like-minded citizens on demand, as opposed to vertical communication from leader to citizen (or vice versa).

Recognizing the superior fit between interactive technology and the social requirements of democracy, several vexing problems of its political fit to democracy arise.

The problem of size remains: it is capable of solution with interactive technology only by limiting the number of participants at any one time. All cannot talk to all (at once) with any technology. Groups of at most 25 or 30 are about the limit with existing telephone conference circuits; much larger than this (even without a technology), and the interaction becomes confused. The question is: How could these limitations be squared with the nature of democracy? Would it be objectionable to develop a citizen technology which would allow only a few to participate? Who would have the privilege and who would have the time?

These questions of time and size obviously are related to the third issue raised by citizen technology, namely, the distribution of benefits. If the real nature of government in America is, as the political scientist Arthur Dahl describes it, a series of nested Chinese boxes, and if the society itself is an unequal ordering of social layers from the active, wealthy, educated, informed on top, to the inactive, uneducated, poor, and uninformed on the bottom, at which point should a citizen technology intervene? Even more important, at which point could the technology successfully intervene?

As we have seen above, the story line of many electronic technologies is that of a new tool in search of a use. The technology, like computers or automated opinion polling, is developed for commercial or military purposes, and a market is sought in the public sector with great claims made for its ultimate benefit to democracy. This often leads to attempts at redefining democracy in order to satisfy the needs of the technology. In this manner, democracy becomes a benign dictatorship of the systems analysts for proponents of computers, or it becomes a dictatorship of "the people" for proponents of mass-participation technology.

I should like to avoid the temptation to fit the political institution to the technology by reviewing briefly the requisites of democracy as we know it in the United States. Once we understand these requisites we can begin to fit the technology to reality in a manner that serves democracy, not destroys it.

NOTES

1. Christopher Lydon, "A Disenchanted Electorate May Stay Home in Droves," New York *Times*, February 1, 1976.

2. William A. Caldwell, *How to Save Urban America* (New York: Signet Books and the Regional Plan Association, 1973).

3. This description is based on an Op-Ed article by Clark McCauley, "Dial M for Mass Transit," New York *Times*, November 5, 1974, as well as personal conversations with McCauley.

4. E.J. Corwin, *Citizen Response: Mass Participation Feedback* (distributed by Mr. Corwin at the annual meetings of the American Association for the Advancement of Science, New York City, 1975).

5. Corwin, op. cit., p. 20.

6. Rita J. Simon, *Public Opinion in America* (Chicago: Rand McNally, 1974).

7. Alfred Sandler, "An Ombudsman for the United States," *The Annals of the American Academy*, May 1968, p. 177.

8. The following description is based upon John D.C. Little et al., "Citizen Feedback Components and Systems," Technical Report No. 76 (Cambridge: Operations Research Center, MIT, 1972).

9. Thomas B. Sheridan, "Technology for Group Dialogue and Social Choice," in *Talking Back*, ed. Ithiel de Sola Poole (Cambridge: MIT Press, 1973), pp. 228-29.

10. *Radical Software* (New York: Gordon and Breach, November 1970).

11. Theodora Sklover, "The Open Door Policy on Television," in *Communication Technology and Social Policy*, ed. George Gerbner, Larry Gross, William Melody (New York: John Wiley, 1973), Chapter 21. See also Federal Communications Commission, *Cable Rules and Regulations* (February 12, 1972).

12. Pamela Doty, "Public Access Cable TV: Programming," *Journal of Communications* (Summer 1975).

13. Alan Wurtzel, "Public Access Cable TV: Programming," *Journal of Communications* (Summer 1975).

14. Rudy Bretz, "Public Access Cable TV: Audiences," *Journal of Communications* (Summer 1975).

15. Bretz, ibid.

16. Doty, op. cit.

17. Bretz, op. cit.

18. Ithiel de Sola Poole, "Citizen Feedback in Political Philosophy," in Poole, *Talking Back*, pp. 242-43.

19. Angus Campbell et al., *The American Voter* (New York: John Wiley, 1964), p. 51.

20. Harold Mendelsohn, "The Neglected Majority," in Poole, *Talking Back*, p. 35. Mendelsohn attributes low educational TV viewing by working class adults to the dominance of middle class people in all media. He proposes a working class television, similar to cable public access.

21. J.C.R. Licklider, "Televistas: Looking Ahead Through Side Windows" in *Social Speculations*, ed. Richard Kostelanetz (New York: W.R. Morrow, 1971), p. 159.

22. For a detailed discussion of such systems in the public sector see Kenneth Laudon, *Computers and Bureaucratic Reform* (New York: John Wiley, 1974).

23. For a description of this project see Caldwell, op. cit.

24. Edward Sofen, *The Miami Experiment* (Bloomington, Indiana: Indiana University Press, 1963).

25. Laudon, op. cit., Chapter 4.

26. The following description is based on D.J. Alesch, "Intergovernmental Communication in the New York-New Jersey-Connecticut Metropolitan Region" (Santa Monica: Rand Corporation R-977-MRC, May 1972), and upon The Annual Report, 1969, 1970, and 1972 of the Metropolitan Regional Council, in addition to site visits to MRC-TV in the World Trade Center.

3

THE REQUISITES OF
DEMOCRACY

In the assembly of Athens it was possible for Pericles to address directly the 10,000 citizens of Athens—or at least those citizens who chose to attend the assembly. It was possible for each of the citizens in turn to address Pericles, although, to be sure, this was a more difficult and tedious process. Yet it was possible. After nearly 2,500 years of technological development in the West, the size of a modern-day Pericles' audience is almost unlimited. Yet the ability of citizens to talk with other citizens has remained virtually constant while their ability to talk with leaders has shrunk to infinitesimal size. Political dialogue among citizens in modern democracies is largely limited by the strength of the unaided voice as it was 2,000 years ago. Relative to the size of modern democracies, clearly the role of citizen has declined enormously.

If we take as the central problem of any democracy that of organizing the preferences and beliefs of a large number of people into a single, collective choice, and then of translating that collective choice into actual public policy, we are immediately confronted once again with the problems of size, time, and inequality. The classical model of direct democracy offers a practical, if not elegant, solution to these problems: restrict the physical and demographic size of a democracy to city-states, allow only a patrician leisure class to participate in politics, and use the democratic model only where inequality is minimal.[1]

In the classical view, then, democracy was not by any means the most appropriate form of government for all societies. Aristotle points to several related factors that determine the ability of democracies to survive. The larger a society, the more difficult was communication among citizens and between citizens and leaders. Large societies also were more fragmented into interest blocs, which portended great conflict. Normative attachments to the polity would in turn be weaker: citizens would make decisions in their self-interest, as opposed to the collective interest. With the material inequality found in large societies, participation of all citizens would be problematic, if not impossible, at least on equal terms. Democracy, then, was limited in the classical view to societies with no more than 10,000 citizens of roughly equal social standing. In larger societies, some form of oligarchy or despotism was thought inevitable.[2]

The increasing asymmetry between leader and citizen, the declining capacity of citizens to influence, is of course precisely what modern democratic theorists have worried about since the beginning of the eighteenth century, and especially since the first broadly based, large scale, representative democracy, the United States, began. The development of representative legislatures in large Western nations has taxed political philosophers and pamphleteers greatly: the representative legislatures, and the governments in which they were embedded, bore at best a distant relationship to what had been called "democracy." For some, such as Rousseau and Montesquieu, the transition from small city-state to nation-state made democracy in any real sense impossible. Montesquieu writes:

> It is in the nature of a Republic that it should have a small territory; without that, it could scarcely exist. In a large Republic, there are large fortunes and consequently little moderation of spirit; there are trusts too great to be placed in the hands of any single citizen; interests become particularized; a man begins to feel that he can be happy, great, and glorious without his country; and then, that he can become great upon the ruins of his country.[3]

Montesquieu found it natural and good then that large states would be governed by despots, small states by a republican form of democracy. The divergent interests, the impossibility of a rough equality among citizens in large states, all portended conflict so great that any sort of agreement among citizens in large states was impossible. Rousseau in particular emphasized the role of social inequality in wealth, power, and prestige as preempting democracy for large states.[4]

THE CONTEMPORARY VIEW OF DEMOCRACY

The emergence of large nation-states with representative forms of government in the nineteenth and twentieth centuries has led to the reformulation of democratic theory. The role of citizen is largely subsumed within the context of groups, associations, and complex organizations; the citizen participates indirectly in politics through his membership in larger collectivities. Consensus, the process of shaping collective decisions from individual wills, is largely the product of interaction and adjustment among groups.[5]

In the nineteenth century Moisei Ostrogorski was among the first to note the significance of mass political parties based upon universal suffrage. For

Ostrogorski, the new mass party structures that replaced the caucus of notables in parliament became the only vehicle available to a free society for arbitrating conflict:

> Before liberty had become the basis of government, popular opposition and discontent found vent in riots and civil wars. In proportion as the regime of opinion took the place of that of brute force, internal conflicts assumed another character. The adjustment of differences was henceforth left to the free play of moral forces of the nation; conspiracies were to give way to a union of convictions, and revolts to the manifestation of these convictions.[6]

Ostrogorski was highly critical of these new political structures. The new parties for all their public obeisance to the values of universal suffrage and liberty, were privately corrupt, boss-ridden oligarchies controlled by and for the benefit of a few; manipulation of the electorate with false promises and intentional blurring of ideological and political issues in the competition for mass electoral support supplanted rational political dialogue.

Later writers, principally Max Weber, came to accept these features of electoral competition based on mass parties. For Weber the competition of parties for support of the great mass of voters in the center necessarily lessened the differences among parties, and moderated the level of political conflict. The replacement of amateur notables who, according to Burke, participated in politics to promote the public welfare based "upon some principle on which they are all agreed," by professional party bureaucrats motivated by greed and survival served to further moderate the public positions of the new parties.[7]

By the first third of the twentieth century the contemporary descriptions and theory of democracy had fully displaced direct citizen participation. Henceforth institutionalized competition among legitimate parties became the defining characteristic of democracy. Joseph Schumpeter writes:

> To put it differently, we now take the view that the role of the people is to produce a government, or else an intermediate body which in turn will produce a national executive or government. And we define: the democratic method is that institutional arrangement for arriving at political decisions in which individuals acquire power to decide by means of a competitive struggle for the people's vote. . . .
>
> Party and machine politicians are simply the response to the fact that the electoral mass is incapable of action other than a stampede, and they constitute an attempt to regulate political competition exactly similar to the corresponding practices of a trade association.
>
> The psycho-technics of party management and party advertising, slogans and marching tunes, are not accessories. They are the essence of politics. So is the political boss.[8]

Schumpeter's analogy between economic organization and political competition reflected the views of earlier U.S. writers, such as Lincoln Steffens, who wrote, "politics is business. If our political leaders are to always a lot of political merchants, they will supply any demand we may create. Isn't our corrupt government, after all, representative?"[9]

But these views that saw democracy as only institutionalized competition were profoundly disturbing to many because they implied that democracies could easily emerge into tyrannical despotisms in which Schumpeter's "psycho-technics" of one party were so successful that the competition was eliminated. If the electorate was merely a manipulable, fickle mass, so many cattle about to stampede, then the idea of basing public policy on the preferences of citizens was absurd. That is, a kind of mass hysteria manipulated by elites would replace a legitimate consensus based upon the adjustment of real interest. The experience of fascism and other mass phenomena of the 1930s and 1940s only heightened this perception. The possibility of stable party competition seemed shattered by the experience of European societies in which the breakdown of intermediate institutions, for example, the church, community, and professional groups, left citizens more accessible to the new despots of nationalism. Sigmund Neuman writes of the period:

> Resulting from the recent rise of mass democracy and the threatening breakdown of institutions, two elements of crisis loom for modern government. The same elements constitute the historic premises for the new despots. Their primary claim is leadership in the mass state and substitution for shattered institutions.[10]

The rise of fascism and totalitarianism in the Soviet Union, as perhaps no other event, led contemporary writers to further specify the conditions under which stable democracy as an institutionalized competition among parties could exist for long periods of time.

Aided by new empirical tools of analysis, the early electoral studies of Paul Lazarsfeld et al. in the 1940s showed that in the United States, a stable democracy, the voters were not a fickle mass and exhibited instead a large mea-sure of stability in terms of party allegiance across elections, and even across generations. Those who belonged to intermediate institutions, from churches to labor unions, were less likely to switch their votes during the campaign, tended to discuss politics more, and were more knowledgable about politics than nonmembers. Moreover, citizens tended to select membership in intermediate institutions in accordance with their political beliefs. Thus the subgroups to which citizens belong tend to reflect their views.[11] These findings have been collaborated by other more extensive studies of national elections.[12] In addition, the work of Seymour Lipset et al. in its study of democracy within a trade union illustrates how a historical tradition of party competition is supported by a network of social, occupational, and political subgroups.[13]

Hence the second major tenet of the contemporary theory of democracy is that durable party competition is dependent upon the existence and vitality of autonomous subgroups in a society, which mediate between the citizen, political parties, and ultimately the state. The nature of these subgroups varies as to circumstances: they may be intimate social and work groups or large associations such as unions, trade associations, and so forth. Unlike classical theories, large size and material inequality do not prohibit democracy. These problems are overcome by the collection of smaller, more homogeneous communities that make up society. In this view, democracy in huge societies like the United States is a collection of thousands, if not millions, of minidemocracies.

SUBGROUPS AND THE THEORY OF DEMOCRACY

The crucial role which social, religious, and occupational subgroups play in contemporary descriptions of democracy in large nation-states deserves further elaboration. In the first instance, these intermediate groups between citizen and state act as loci of independent opinion formation. They help to crystallize and organize millions of individual preferences into a much smaller number of subgroup preferences. Ideally these intermediate groups approach in function and character the assemblies of Athens: they are small enough to allow face-to-face interaction and a sense of personal identity, and generally are composed of persons of roughly equal social status. Yet they are, in theory at least, big enough to give the average citizen some sense and reality of political power. If a group of community residents bands together and successfully pressures the local government to install a street lamp, each person gains a measure of political power. Even members of the community who do not directly participate in the resident group may come to feel that citizens have some influence over local governors.

As a result, it is thought that these subgroups provide citizens of large, complex nations opportunities for political communication, participation, and a sense of personal efficacy over political matters. Hence these groups act to produce political consensus in its most elementary and classical sense as a converging of citizen preferences through direct interaction.

Through the process of interaction natural leaders arise within these subgroups, and a second crucial function of these intermediate groups is to recruit and train such leaders.[14] These subgroup leaders are generally selected by their peers in accordance with the norms of the group;[15] in turn, these leaders shape and organize the opinions of their constituents.

Such leaders are thought to provide the critical link between national political issues and local communities. One writer in this tradition explains:

> Such critical individuals at the junction points in networks of
> personal influence manifest in modern society a Jeffersonian image

of the ideal grass-roots leaders. That is, they are likely to be active in routine social life, competent in politics, but yet so thoroughly ordinary citizens that they are in fact models or prototypes for the others whom they inform, argue with, and influence in politics. If something like this is the actual case in the factories, farms and neighborhoods of today, then the political wisdom of an apolitical people may consist of an ability to judge among the especially competent and trusted people around them, as well as the theoretically desirable but practically difficult capacity to judge the distant national debate.[16]

The autonomy of subgroups from the state and large political parties, in combination with the existence of peer-selected leaders, serves to protect the individual citizen from direct mobilization by the state. Subgroup leaders serve as interpreters for the subgroup with regard to political news and events, and they tend to be respected by members for their political judgments.

Usually in concert with other like-minded subgroups, most often through the interaction of subgroup leaders, intermediate groups function to mobilize their members at appropriate moments in political life to impress upon larger political entities, parties, and the state, the views of their constituents. This process of coalition formation among subgroups and the influence of such coalitions upon larger political entities is crucial to the operation of modern complex democracies, for it is the only path, however indirect, through which citizens can have a continuing influence over specific collective decisions. While it is true that universal suffrage allows citizens in a democracy direct access to societal decision makers, this access occurs at infrequent intervals and is continually vitiated by the competition of mass parties. Only the most general and broadly defined consensus can emerge from universal suffrage, while the specification of consensus into actual policies requires interaction between societal leaders and subgroups.[17]

In the view of one contemporary theorist, William Kornhauser, the dual nature of social subgroups as anchors of public opinion and mobilizers of citizen influence effectively prevents totalitarianism:

> Pluralist society requires accessible elites and unavailable non-elites if it is to sustain its freedom and diversity—as in liberal democracies. Elites are accessible in that competition among independent groups opens many channels of communication and power. The population is unavailable in that people possess multiple commitments to diverse and autonomous groups. The mobilization of a population bound by multiple commitments would require the breaking up of large numbers of independent organizations, as totalitarian movements have sought to do.[18]

FIGURE 1

A Communication Tree View of Representative Polities

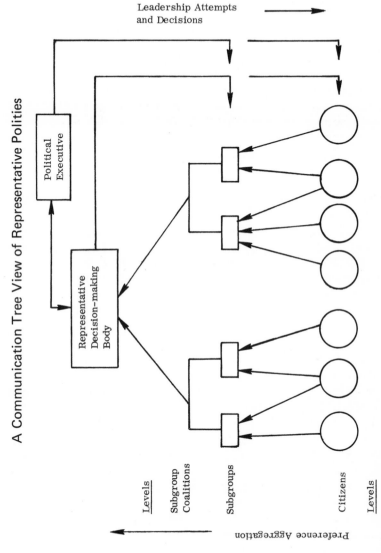

Source: Compiled by the author.

The pictorial view of modern democracies which emerges from the above discussion is something like a "communication tree," which percolates individual preferences upwards through several communities and subgroupings (see Figure 1).

In this simplified pictorial model citizens at the lowest level are separated into subgroups in accordance with their beliefs and interests, with many citizens having multiple affiliations. Through interaction, the most elementary kind of consensus is produced, and subgroup leaders (either formal or informal) emerge. Through interaction with other subgroup leaders, coalitions among subgroups develop, which lead to influence attempts on representative bodies and political executives. Political parties, an intermediate level of organization, typically form around subgroup blocks in relatively stable patterns. While this simplified model has only three levels, in reality there may be as many as 10 or 15 levels between citizens and decision makers.[19]

POLITICAL PROCESS IN LARGE DEMOCRACIES

The political process, even in this simplified model, is much more complex than suggested by classical models of democracy based upon open assemblies of citizens. Here it is highly differentiated and multitiered, whereas in classical models the political process has a single tier (the assembly) and is less specialized (citizens actually were decision makers). In the contemporary theory and practice of large democracies, consensus emerges from a combination of processes which occur at different times and places. The simple convergence of opinion through direct interaction still occurs but in small subgroups—not the polity as a whole. An upward process of coalition formation which aggregates subgroup preferences occurs but does not directly involve the citizen as much as his informal leaders. Leadership, the direct attempts of formal officials to alter the emerging consensus, completes the process. Let us assume that this model of modern, large democracies developed in the last two decades is a reasonably accurate outline of how such democracies work. And let us ask how the central problems faced by such a democracy—size, time, and inequality—are solved in practice.

The problem of size is partly solved in a formal sense by splitting up the decision making in society among the many levels of national, state, and local government. At an informal level the problem is solved by allowing citizens to participate directly in small groups which, in turn, it is thought, can effect changes in formal government policy. Necessarily this means the average person feels rather distant from decisions made at national, state, and even local levels. Even in small towns of 100,000 residents, the social distance between one's block association and the mayor is apt to be large and involve traversing several tiers of political structure. With a growing recognition of how great is this distance between small group and formal government, we should not be surprised at the following picture of alienation produced by Louis Harris over the last decade:[20]

Statement	Percentage Agreeing			
	1966	1968	1971	1972
What you think doesn't count much	39%	42%	44%	53%
The people running the country don't really care what happens to people like yourself	28	36	41	50
You feel left out of things around you	9	12	20	25

The problem of time is partially solved by the necessarily slow pace of decision making in modern democracies. The process of developing a public policy position on a major piece of legislation for even the large subgroups (labor, business, and professional groups) may take several months; agreement among these interest groups may take several years. The snail's pace of decision making allows, on the other hand, a broader range of interests to be included.

Yet, other dimensions of the time problem are obviously troublesome. The amount of time the average person can devote to participation is highly limited; all cannot talk to all about even a single issue in a society of millions or cities of thousands. The practical, though not elegant, solution found in all large democracies is a very steep interest gradient. In presidential election years, more than 40 percent of the electorate does not care very much or at all about the outcome; this number has increased steadily since 1956 with a corresponding drop in voter turnout at the polls from 73 percent to 55 percent by 1972. In local and and state elections, participation and interest are about 50 percent less than in national elections.

When considering the more active forms of political participation such as actually working on a campaign, in no election since 1956 has more than 7 percent of the electorate ever attended political rallies, meetings, or dinners.[21]

Briefly then, the personal dimensions of the time problem, the limitations on individual ability to participate politically and even to follow political arguments in newspapers and books, is functionally solved by limiting interest in politics to those who have the inclination, leisure time, interest, and skills. Necessarily, this is a small number composed of perhaps 10 percent of the electorate. This compares poorly to the 24 percent of adult Americans (32 million) who regularly read the daily newspaper astrology columns.[22]

Aside from growing levels of alienation and political withdrawal, the problem of inequality stands out as the most severe in large democracies.

The problem of political inequality is formally solved in this model of democracy by universal suffrage. Yet insofar as there is social inequality in the distribution of money and political skills, and insofar as these resources are important for political influence in between elections, the problem of inequality remains largely unresolved. Typically it is seen as a problem of income distribution among individual citizens. Doris Kearns, a political scientist, citing the concentration of income and wealth among the top corporations and individuals writes:

> In my view, unless this concentration of economic resources can be dispersed, there is little chance of breaking up political concentrations of power. Priority attention must be given, therefore, to the dispersal of economic power through vigorous enforcement of antitrust laws, redistribution of income, and reform of the tax structure. Only with these changes can we begin slowly to recreate competitive social context within which American democracy will once more flourish.[23]

Such views that call for income distribution are widespread. They have been widespread for at least 40 years, since the depression. They have had little impact on the reality of concentrated wealth and almost no impact on political inequality. If the past is any guide, they will continue to have little impact.

We must ask, if wealth were equally distributed and if college diplomas were handed out at birth like social security numbers, would it make any political difference? Would the one-half of the population whose income goes up suddenly develop an interest in politics? Would a population of college graduates believe itself closer to political decision making? Would it in fact be closer? And if these measures did result in heightened interest, broadly spread political skills, and greater leisure time for politics, could the existing political democracy handle the demand for participation?

The answer to most of these questions is probably no. The social benefits of income and education redistribution (such as a greater degree of social justice) are not easily translatable into political benefits for large democracies. The problems of time, size, and political inequality would still be with us.

CRITICAL VIEWS

The argument seems to have reached an impasse. The practical solutions to the problems of time, size, and political inequality developed in large-scale modern democracies lead to undesirable levels of withdrawal, alienation, and cynicism. A redistribution of social resources will not likely bring the average citizen closer to decision making, increase his interest in politics, or permit direct participation in politics. Indeed, just the opposite might happen: a large number of newly active citizens competing for a limited number of influence channels.

A part of this impasse results from the way we have framed the answers to the key problems of democracy. Admittedly, in large-scale democracies the average citizen is distant from decision making, unlikely to have the time or interest in more participation, and just as often does not have the resources or skills for much influence. We have focused largely on the problem of how to bring the vast numbers of individual citizens closer to political decision making. But it does not seem the problem is solvable on this level. Briefly, there most likely is no way in a large democracy to bring citizens as individuals closer to political decision making.

Perhaps the most poignant fault in modern democracies like the United States is not that large numbers of citizens are inactive, apathetic, and cynical. Perhaps the most significant loss is that groups of citizens who are interested, involved, and active nevertheless lose out in the political competition to the much more powerful interest blocs.

This suggests a different line of criticism and perhaps some new solutions. The more fundamental criticism to be made of this contemporary model of democracy is that the subgroup structure itself, the institutional infrastructure, is defunct, or at least highly inefficient. Three specific arguments are important here.

Societal Subgroups Are Oligarchic

The experience of most people who are members of unions, professional associations, church groups, business associations and other voluntary, private associations is that at the head of each a small body of men with long tenure rule without organized opposition. Modern research on oligarchy in private associations only has confirmed Robert Michels' findings that "whoever says organization says oligarchy."[24] Once elected to the offices of large private associations, leaders monopolize the means of political communication, seek to maintain their new higher status by destroying opposition, and through their command of an army of bureaucrats loyal to them alone, are able to perpetuate their reign. Followers and members, less educated in the ways of political combat, apathetic because they sense their voices will not be heard, and uninterested because of competing demands on their time and resources, are forever a captive flock.

To be sure, not all societal subgroups can be so characterized. Many of the subgroups to which we belong are small enough to permit direct face-to-face interaction with other members and leaders, and are less formalized than large private associations. Community-based groups, such as school PTAs, tenant associations, church congregations, sports groups, and the like, are more homogeneous and consensual. Yet they are equally incapable of affecting larger political processes which demand, in the views of one critic, Theodore Lowi, the formation of peak associations to conduct political combat:

> From the NAM and the U.S. Chamber of Commerce and all the State Chambers of Commerce, to the Farm Bureau Federation, to the Federation of Jewish Philanthropies and the Council of Churches, to the AFL-CIO, we have layer upon layer of "peak associations," which exist to institutionalize relations among constituent groups. Each peak association and every major interest group started out as a coalition that eventually perpetrated itself by the development of a central administrative core.[25]

While the countless small associations to which citizens belong may serve as anchors of citizen views, inhibiting mass tendencies and organizing citizen opinions, they are politically efficacious only insofar as they coalesce into larger, oligarchic institutions. It is largely agreed that the results of this pattern are the adoption of politics at odds with citizen desires, apathy, and cynicism toward both private and public political institutions.

The consequences of peak associations upon less formal local subgroups vary in accordance with circumstances. In many cases, depending on the degree of penetration of local groups by peak associations, even the stabilizing and crystallizing functions of private   associations are disturbed. Duverger writes of European working-class parties based upon local cells:

> Instead of a body intended for the winning of votes, for grouping the representatives, and for maintaining contact between them and their electors, the political party becomes an instrument of agitation, of propaganda, of discipline, and, if necessary, of clandestine action. . . .[26]

In the United States, Grant McConnell found in his study of private associations a similar lack of autonomy with respect to opinion formation:

> The remarkable fact about private government, then, is not that it is oligarchic but that it generally lacks the limitations that guard against tyranny and injustice to minorities and individuals. . . . Certainly a greater degree of homogeneity is possible in a private association than in a nation. . . .Nevertheless the difference is one of degree, and the problems of politics, of reconciling differences, and of limiting political power remain. The record of private associations in dealing with these problems gives little justification for the wishful view that the private association is the natural home of democracy.[27]

In the eyes of many critics, then, the image of modern democracies composed of Jeffersonian, autonomous groups and communities is simply unrealistic. The problems of political democracy simply reappear at a different level.

Societal Subgroups Are Fragmented and Isolated

The ability of local subgroups to coalesce into larger, more effective, yet democratic entities is severely limited by the primitive tools of communication, coordination, and organization available to such groups. The political landscape as a result is littered with the fragments of once-potent local groups whose members are overcome with frustration at trying to effect larger political realities. Counterbalancing the emergence of peak associations without any grass roots are thousands of like-minded local subgroups incapable of developing effective coalition. Indeed, these are two aspects of the same dilemma: oligarchical effectiveness versus grass-roots localism.

The 1960s was a decade fairly overrun with grass-roots organization in civil rights, antiwar, and religious areas. Characterized by one student as decentralized and segmented "movement organizations" they developed a surprising amount of power and pressure toward changing established institutions.[28] Yet they were most criticized for their inability to develop regional, state, and national linkages suitable for pressing grievances to systematic resolution.

Most analysts of grass-roots organizations in this period point to the militancy of these groups as a source of schisms and ultimate weakness; others to the instability—both psychological and social—of the by-and-large youthful members.[29] Quite often the local grass-roots organizations came into direct field conflict with the more established peak organizations. This clearly happened throughout the South in the early 1960s between the Southern Christian Leadership Conference (SCLC) and local voter registration groups.[30]

Less well recognized as a source of weakness for grass-roots groups is their inability to coordinate activities even at the local level. One participant comments on problems of community organizations in the South:

> Our local leader really gave us and especially me hell for causing so many problems. . . .There is a lack of communication (e.g., Friday night we had a rally in the park without getting final approval from the local leaders—my fault). I think the main problem is lack of communication. A lot of this is due to the factor that none of them has enough time to be in constant contact with us and I can't get in contact with them.[31]

These problems of coordination were not confined to militant, ideological, or youthful grass-roots movements alone. In the urban North the same weakness developed among tenant groups and block associations who sought nothing more radical than rent reduction, garbage collection, and hot running water. The ability of these groups to persuade mayors, councilmen, and city agencies to act on these problems depends in large measure on the simultaneous activation of tenants in several buildings and in many neighborhoods. In the 1960s, one of the few coordination tools available to such local groups was the mass media which, in turn, set definite limits on community organization.

> Low-income groups may be thought of as politically impoverished. . . . To the extent that a successful protest depends on appealing to . . . other groups in the community, publicity through the public media will set limits of how far that protest activity will go towards success. If the communications media either ignore the protest or play it down, it will not succeed.[32]

In competition with the more oligarchic associations of landlords, tenant groups are far less successful in mobilizing members and impressing their views on elected officials. The difficulty of establishing regular communication and coordination channels among grass-roots subgroups is both a principle cause of their weakness and a fundamental contributor to the emergence of oligarchies. In such a manner, local subgroups are prevented from having much influence over larger political affairs. And insofar as local subgroups coalesce into existing peak organizations, or create new ones in their place, so do they lose the commitment, energy, and participation of local members which once made them strong.[33]

Important Interests Are Not Represented

Perhaps the most persistent criticism of modern democracies is that important interests and groups are not represented in the consensus-building process and in the societal decisions that result. In large measure this is simply due to the persistent inequalities in money and status that characterize the larger society. Universal suffrage and electoral competition among parties overcome to some extent these inequalities. However, elections and voting produce only the most general and broad kind of consensus. The specification of electoral consensus into actual policies generally requires the sustained long-term organization of interests and groups. It is here that money and status inequalities distort consensus building.

One example should suffice. The political organization we examine in this book has about 10,000 members drawn from predominantly upper-middle-class professional backgrounds. Its annual budget is $100,000 or about $11 a member on the average. It is capable of maintaining a permanent staff of lobbyists at the state capitol, backed up by a permanent state headquarters staff. With support of its highly educated membership, the permanent organization can call forth a deluge of letters, telegrams, reports, and testimony for the benefit of state legislators. In an adjoining state, the largest welfare rights organization in the country with a welfare population of over 2 million has approximately 10,000 dues-paying members with a member budget of $20,000. Most of this money is spent on a volunteer coordinating staff in a large city; lobbying efforts at the state capital are episodic and generally involve busing members to the capital for a one day "shock" effort. The organization tends to be dominated by one or two charismatic leaders in its lobbying efforts; although local chapters within major cities have been successful in changing local administration of welfare, they have made little impact on legislation.[34]

Inequality in status, which often parallels material inequality, is another distorting effect on consensus-building. When 150 prominent scientists protest federal government affirmative action policies, it is duly reported in the New York *Times*, front page.[35] The protests of organized women's groups are likely to be found on the society pages. As Lipsky notes of urban community groups, they

> seldom have enough people of high status to work for their proposals. Good causes sometimes attract such people, but seldom for long. Therefore protest groups hardly ever have the expertise and experience they need including professionals, in such fields as law, architecture, accounting, education, and how to get government money.[36]

The part-time organizational skills lent to certain community groups by young professionals and students are by their very nature ephemeral and hardly a match for the paid political professionals available to wealthier groups.

The consequence of persistent inequality is that in the competition of interest groups, those with less money and status, but especially those with less organization, lose out. Inevitably the members of such groups either lose interest in a hopeless cause, or resort to "cheaper" political combat tactics such as demonstrations, sit-ins, and other highly visible, often violent, available techniques. Apathy and resignation, spiced by the "revolutionary judo" appropriate to demonstration democracy, develop together.[37]

Yet the existence of mere inequality does not alone explain the non-representation of important interests and groups. Mediating between inequality and political influence is the nature of political organization itself. The current close association between material and status wealth and the tools of political organization is the heart of the problem: current techniques of organization and influence are priced above the resources of important subgroups and interests.

THE REQUISITES OF DEMOCRACY

Democracy does not require that everyone should participate in the decisions that affect their lives, for there are too many decisions in too many places taken at different times. Promising delivery from this fact of large-scale democracies through technological or other gimmickry is likely to increase withdrawal, alienation, and cynicism—not relieve it.

The minimal requisites of a plural democracy composed of many groups and interests are that interested and active citizens be capable of expressing their views within these smaller subgroups; that, in turn, these smaller subgroups have the means to coalesce into larger coalitions of like-minded groups; and that the means or tools of political organization be sufficiently widespread and inexpensive so that social inequality per se does not determine the outcome of political competition.

If these are the necessary requisites of a plural democracy, they may not themselves be sufficient. Other requisites such as norms of tolerence, checks and balances in the formal organization of power, and a legal-historical tradition of limited state power, may also be thought of as necessary.

Yet, in crucial respects, these other conditions rely on the more fundamental requisites outlined above. Norms of tolerance develop from the concerted political organization of minority groups who demand no less; checks and balances, and legal-historical definitions of the role of the state are maintained through the intervention of organized groups when these principles are violated.

THE ROLE OF CITIZEN TECHNOLOGY

The proper role of any new citizen technology is not to replace the existing democratic institutions with an engineering nightmare called "the wired nation." The requisites of democracy are to some extent fulfilled in U.S. society. There are indeed some politically powerful loose coalitions on the national scene which are composed of local, active subgroups. Yet more often, as pointed out above, these groups tend to be oligarchic internally or to become so with time; just as often local subgroups form with no possibility of linking up with other like-minded groups in other parts of the nation or even within the same state.

The question to answer, then, is whether a technology can be developed that might enhance the existing democratic institutions.

This large question has three related facets. First, can a technology be designed that would enhance the ability of existing local community groups to coordinate activities and form coalitions despite large geographical and social dispersion? Second, will the use of this technology lessen the functional utility of peak associations and oligarchies that currently dominate the political landscape? Put another way, can existing oligarchies be weakened, nascent oligarchies prevented, and competition with opposing oligarchies "tilted" in favor of grass-roots organizations? Third, can the technology be made sufficiently cheap and its use sufficiently simple so as to weaken the close association between social resources (money and education) and political influence?

TECHNOLOGICAL REQUISITES

If this is the proper role of a citizen technology, the next question is, what sort of technology can meet these requirements? Clearly, more and larger computers in the hands of government bureaucrats, or a computer in every living room, do not seem to provide what is wanted. Neither are more television channels—cable or not—required. These technologies strengthen the vertical linkage between leaders and the led. Whatever benefits these developments will produce for the collection of better information on citizens, a "cashless" society, or simply the selling of soap, they do not seem to advance the requisites of democracy.

The family of technologies we labelled interactive that strengthen the horizontal linkages of communication among like-minded persons offer more of what is wanted. Unfortunately, these interactive technologies are not well developed and certainly are not inexpensive. The only exception is the telephone conference call, which is reasonably developed, widespread, and cheap. For these reasons, telephone conferencing was chosen as the basis of the experiment reported in Chapter 4.

EXPERIMENTAL DESIGN REQUISITES

The questions outlined above cannot be explored any further in theory but require empirical inquiry and exploration. The primitive nature of inter-active technology, and a limited research budget augured for a one-time explora-tory study on a small scale. Rather than attempt a large-scale study involving a small town or city, which necessarily would have fragmented our limited resources and reduced the amount of useful information we could collect, we decided instead to explore in depth the consequences of using citizen technology in a large, grassroots organization of 10,000 members. This strategy does not answer all the questions which might be raised about citizen technology. Yet, as we will see, it is sufficient to explore the more significant problems.

NOTES

1. One who has taught me much about democracy is Robert A. Dahl. On these points see his *After the Revolution?* (New Haven: Yale University Press, 1970), Chapter 2. Also by the same author, *Size and Democracy* (Stanford: Stanford University Press, 1973).

2. *Aristotle: The Politics*, trans. T.A. Sinclair. (Baltimore: Penguin Books, 1962), book 3, Chapter 2.

3. Charles-Louis De Montesquieu, *De l'Esprit des Lois* (Paris, 1961), vol. 1, book 8, p. 181, trans. and cited in Dahl, *Size and Democracy*, p. 7.

4. Jean-Jacques Rousseau, *The Social Contract*, book 3, part 4, "Of Democracy": "There too should be considerable equality in fortune and rank, for otherwise there will not be long equality in rights and authority."

5. One of the better extended treatments of changes in the role of citizen is Sheldon Wolin, *Politics and Vision* (Boston: Little, Brown, 1960).

6. M. Ostrogorski, *Democracy and the Organization of Political Parties*, ed. and abridged by Seymour Martin Lipset (New York: Anchor Books, 1964), p. 61.

7. See Weber's essay, "Politics as a Vocation," in *From Max Weber*, trans. and ed. H.H. Gerth and C. Wright Mills (New York: Oxford University Press, 1958).

8. Joseph A. Schumpeter, *Capitalism, Socialism and Democracy* (New York: Harper and Row, 1962), pp. 269, 283.

9. Lincoln Steffens, *The Shame of the City* (New York: Hill and Wang, 1957), pp. 5-6.

10. Sigmund Neuman, *Permanent Revolution* (New York: Praeger, 1965), p. 3.

11. Bernard Berelson, Paul Lazersfeld, and William McPhee, *Voting* (Chicago: University of Chicago Press, 1966), Chapters 3 and 6.

12. Angus Campbell et al., *The American Voter* (New York: John Wiley, 1964). Jerome Clubb and Howard Allen, *Electoral Change and Stability in American Political History* (New York: Free Press, 1971). James Sundquist, *Dynamics of the Party System* (Washington D.C.: The Brookings Institution, 1973). Each of these works concludes that voter realignments are not fickle or short-term but rather occur because of long-term shifts in voter identification and interest group alignments.

13. Seymour Lipset, Martin Trow, and James Coleman, *Union Democracy* (New York: Anchor Books, 1962).

14. Lipset et al., *Union Democracy* remains one of the best descriptions of how subgroups are useful for leader recruitment. See Chapters 10 and 11.

15. George Homans, *The Human Group* (New York: Harcourt, Brace, Jovanovich, 1950). A more systematic treatment of subgroup leaders can be found in Terence Hopkins, *The Exercise of Influence in Small Groups* (New Jersey: Bedminister Press, 1964).

16. Berelson et al., *Voting*, p. 115.

17. For a critical study of the role played by societal subgroups and interests in the specifications of societal decisions, see Grant McConnell, *Private Power and American Democracy* (New York: Vintage Books, 1966). For an earlier, but still relevant study, see Philip Selznick, *TVA and the Grass Roots* (Berkeley: University of California Press, 1949). These studies focus on, respectively, national and regional private subgroups in the policy formation and decision-making process. For a vew of the same process in cities, see Edward C. Banfield, *Political Influence* (New York: Free Press, 1965). A much more detailed study of the process in New York City is Wallace Sayre and Herbert Kaufman, *Governing New York City* (New York: Russell Sage Foundation, 1960). The latter work is very informative of microscale community subgroup influence over city policy.

18. William Kornhauser, *The Politics of Mass Society* (New York: Free Press, 1965), p. 41.

19. For further discussion of this model and its communication aspects see Amitai Etzioni, Kenneth Laudon, and Sara Lipson, "Participatory Technology: The Minerva Communications Tree," *The Journal of Communications* (Summer 1975).

20. Cited in *Talking Back*, ed. Ithiel de Sola Poole (Cambridge: MIT Press, 1973), p. 1.

21. Angus Campbell et al., *The American Voter*, Chapter 4. For more recent data see the reports of Christopher Lydon, "A Disenchanted Electorate May Stay Home In Droves," New York *Times*, February 1, 1976.

22. According to a Gallup poll reported in New York *Times*, October 19, 1975.

23. See Doris Kearns, "Reforming Government: Now and in the Future," *American Issues Forum* (distributed by United Press International, December 1975).

24. Robert Michels, *Political Parties* (New York: Free Press, 1961), p. 365.

25. Theodore J. Lowi, *The End of Liberalism* (New York: W.W. Norton, 1969), p. 40.

26. Maurice Duverger, *Political Parties*, trans. Barbara and Robert North (New York: John Wiley, 1967), p. 361.

27. Grand McConnell, *Private Power and American Democracy*, p. 154.

28. One of the best structural treatments of movement organizations which avoids psychologizing the participants is Luther Gerlach and Virginia Hines, *People, Power and Change: Movements of Social Transformation* (New York: Bobbs-Merrill, 1970).

29. For a sociological view that analyses the impact of militancy upon grass-roots stability, see Mayer N. Zald and Roberta Ash, "Social Movement Organization: Growth, Decay and Change," *Social Forces* 44 (1966). For a more psychological view, see Hans Toch, *The Social Psychology of Social Movements* (Indianapolis: Bobbs-Merrill, 1965). For the role of youth in modern movements, see Kenneth Keniston, *Young Radicals* (New York: Harcourt, Brace and World, 1968).

30. N.J. Demerath, Gerald Marwell, and Michael Aiken, *Dynamics of Idealism* (San Francisco: Jossey-Bass, 1969), Chapter 4.

31. Cited in Demerath et al., *Dynamics of Idealism*, p. 74.

32. Michel Lipsky, "Rent Strikes: Poor Man's Weapon," *Transaction* (February 1967): 10, 12.

33. Long-term studies of grass-roots groups and their coalitions are scarce. For one study see Sheldon Messinger, "Organizational Transformation: the Study of a Declining Social Movement," *American Sociological Review* 20, 155: 3-10.

34. "National Welfare Rights Organization City-Wide," New York *Times*, April 9, 1972.

35. See New York *Times*, December 15, 1974.

36. Michel Lipsky, "Rent Strikes," p. 13.

37. For a study of the role of demonstration in modern democracies see Amitai Etzioni, *Demonstration Democracy* (New York: Gordon and Breach, 1970). The term "revolutionary judo" was coined by Gerlach and Hines, op. cit., to describe protest tactics which seek to use the values of established groups as a lever of social change.

4

AN EXPERIMENT WITH
CITIZEN TECHNOLOGY

This chapter describes the results of an experiment with citizen technology designed along the lines set forth in the last chapter. Before we report the results, however, it is necessary that we develop some criteria of "success" for evaluating the experiment. Without these, we might never know whether or how well the experiment worked. The previous chapter provides the outlines of some criteria.

The first criterion is that the technology must enhance the ability of local groups to coordinate points of view and develop coalitions to assure adoption of these points of view. Put in other words, the technology must function to increase the amount of consensus among local groups on, say, what are the important issues in a debate, or what tactics should be adopted. By *enhance* we mean the technology must be more than a functional replacement for what existed before. It has to provide a new communications link where none existed previously. The mere replacement of existing techniques of politcal organization, such as letter writing, rallies, conventions, caucuses, and the like, is of little interest here. The technology must provide something not possible with these existing techniques, and in this sense enhance the art of political technique.

The second criterion is that citizen technology, in order to be successful, will have to have some real political consequences. We are not interested in increasing communication among local groups for the fun of it or to find yet another application for the modern transistor. The technology has to be organized in such a fashion that it would make some clear-cut difference for political decision making. Anything less, and we would be talking about gimmicks that in the end intelligent people would clearly reject. Among the more important questions here are: Can the technology increase the real power of local groups and how? Was the power of an existing oligarchy weakened?

The third criterion is that the technology must be cheap enough and skills in its use sufficiently widespread that ordinary citizens and groups can comfortably use it. We are not interested here in developing a citizen technology for college graduates or computer scientists alone. Neither are we interested in technologies useful only to large corporations, universities, or government bodies who possess the requisite skills and resources. These groups no doubt could make use of much simpler citizen technologies, and, in any event, could not be prevented from using the technology. Yet the idea here is to develop a technology capable of widespread use by less institutionalized groups in a democracy, groups that do not typically possess a great deal of technical expertise.

While these three criteria provide the principal basis for evaluating the experiment, other more subjective criteria are important also. For instance, if people who use the technology perceive it to be cumbersome, awkward, or of poor technical quality, then it is unlikely to be used regardless of its political consequences. If the kind of interaction fostered by a citizen technology is perceived as less effective than, say, a face-to-face meeting around a seminar table, then regardless of its "objective" contribution to democracy, the technology might find little use. Briefly, the social-psychological dynamics of using the technology are important and should be a part of its evaluation.

RESEARCH SETTING

Several experiments in citizen technology—as outlined in Chapter 2—have involved experimentation with the democratic process in a town, city, or region of the United States. This may be appropriate for plans that use opinion polls or television broadcasts, the intention of which is to increase involvement of citizens in the existing local government. For several reasons, it is not an appropriate setting for our experiment. As our intention is to alter the distribution of power out of centralized hands to other levels, one is hard-pressed to imagine mayors, county managers, and local political forces lining up to subscribe. While it might be possible to bring about such change in an operating governmental unit, the design is sufficiently untried so that failure is just as likely. Potentially it could be taken over by these local forces and made a mockery of its intention or simply fizzle, as did other experiments that began with ambitions much larger than delivery capacity. Even with the best of intentions, a local elected official would be irresponsible to experiment with the democratic process involving important public decisions by using a scheme never tested before. Coupled with these substantive issues is the problem of evaluating research in large-scale settings. In previous experiments the design was of such large scope that the evaluation of its effects was sloppy and haphazard.

These factors augur, then, for a research setting smaller than a typical governmental unit, yet larger than a small group. This suggested a large organization with political processes roughly analogous to those of a political democracy.

The organization had to meet three criteria. First it would have to be of sufficient geographic and demographic size that its members could not (and in fact, did not) meet together often. This meant the organization had to face the same problems of size and limited time commitment of its members as found in larger plural democracies—albeit on a smaller scale.

Second, the organization would have to be pluralistic in social character. That is, composed of many, smaller and independent subunits or local chapters. Third, it would have to possess a historical tradition of commitment to democracy, along with the appropriate official values and social norms (such as tolerance of diverse views).

In the world of organizations those meeting the criteria of pluralism and internal democracy, of course, are deviant cases. Perhaps a few unions in the United States might fulfill these criteria; but beyond that, most private and public organizations are found to be oligarchic and centralized. However, we should not be too impressed by the deviant nature of the organization needed, inasmuch as, in a world of 250 nations, democracy is also a deviant case. Once again, the point of our experiment is not to show how totalitarian regimes can be technologically transformed into democratic utopias, but rather to show how existing democracies can be strengthened.

Several municipal unions and a public interest association in New York City offered to participate in the experiment, but none met all the above criteria. One organization in New Jersey did meet the criteria: the state League of Women Voters.

The League of Women Voters of the State of New Jersey, is a state-wide organization of 10,000 women. The membership is organized into 96 local chapters, each of which independently elects its own president and board members. The local chapters are separated by distances of up to 300 miles. The membership as a whole is, then, too large and dispersed to meet comfortably in a single location on a regular basis. A biannual state convention of 300 locally elected delegates is the only statewide forum.

The New Jersey League was one of the founding chapters of the National League, established in 1919 by the National American Woman Suffrage Association under the leadership of Carrie Chapman Catt. Envisaged as a federated organization of state chapters, each in turn, with local chapters, the original program of the League called for efforts in the areas of improving U.S. citizenship, protection of women in industry, new food and drug laws, and improvement of election laws. At various times and places, the League has advocated adoption of the petition, initiative, recall, and referendum to curb the power of professional politicans; and short ballots, research bureaus, and "Schools for Citizenship" to better inform the electorate. While the League has created an image of itself as an election watchdog and a source of nonpartisan political information, increasingly, most of its resources have gone for lobbying in support of specific legislative proposals. In recent years, for instance, the New Jersey State League has lobbied the public and also the state government in support of a regional transportation planning bill, an income tax bill to replace reliance on property taxes for school funding, fair housing legislation, consumer protection laws, and other legislation from welfare reform to administration of justice reform.

The long tradition of commitment to democracy in the larger society is mirrored by its ongoing internal democracy and pluralism. Local and state officers are elected by secret balloting of the membership. Local chapters must meet the requirements of the state constitution, and contribute a certain percentage of dues to the state, but in most other matters are largely independent to pursue local activities.

On the criteria of size, pluralism, and internal democracy, the League provides an appropriate setting for our experiment. Yet in several respects it is obviously not entirely analogous to a political democracy. There are no long-standing political parties in the League; factions of short duration form around candidates for office. Like most private associations, from church groups to labor unions, the League is highly homogeneous in social character. It is unlike the heterogeneous U.S. society, and more like that of Sweden or Denmark. The League membership is comparatively wealthy, educated, and of higher prestige than the U.S. population as a whole. These features mean that extrapolation from our results to other organizations or societies must be done with caution. (We discuss these problems in Chapter 5.) These problems would arise, of course, no matter what organization was chosen: none could be considered an exact replica of U.S. society. Yet, in the important respects outlined above—size, pluralism, internal democracy—the League suffices for an exploratory study.

CRITICAL MOMENTS: A DECISION

In the life of most organizations—as well as most societies that are democratic—critical moments of intense political interest, activity, partisanship, and debate are infrequent. A presidential election every four years is such a moment in the United States; few doubt that were these elections more frequent, not only would citizens quickly become bored and tired, but politicians would have little time and even less energy to govern. Most decisions of government are of intense interest only to smaller groups directly affected.

In the League, a critical moment occurs every two years when its program is decided. The program usually consists of a set of 12 issues selected from a larger number of issues that the League will either study or take some action on. Deciding on a program—much like a national agenda or budget—essentially allocates the League's resources, talents, and energy for a two-year period. The importance of this for a voluntary association lies in the fact that membership support, both financial and personal, depends on how well the program reflects the desires of members.

The program itself is divided into two sets of issues. The first is a smaller set of four issues which the League has studied for several years, developed reports and briefings for members, and developed some action proposals. The action taken may be lobbying efforts in the state capitol, publicity campaigns within local districts, or public education programs. Usually all three are involved in this set of "action" issues.

A larger list of eight "study" issues is selected every two years. These issues become the basis of internal education programs in which state-wide committees prepare reports for local chapters and members to discuss. From the discusssion at local levels, a final report with recommendations for specific League actions is prepared.

Because of the importance of the program decision to the League, and the resulting member involvement and interest, we have selected this organizational moment as the time of intervention to test a citizen technology.

PRETECHNOLOGY DECISION MAKING

The importance of selecting a League program is reflected in the time, organizational resources, and decision method used to develop what is called a program consensus. The decision requires three months, the energies of the entire state-level staff, as well as the 96 local presidents. The traditional decision process can be seen as five steps, beginning in early January of a program selection year when the state board directs local chapters to discuss ideas offered by local members for creating the new program. In large chapters, groups of 10 to 20 women may meet in small units, but the typical pattern is general membership meetings in January to develop member suggestions. Local boards summarize the views of members and file written reports with the state board enumerating those issues desired and specifically not desired by the members (the latter are typically old program items of which the members are tired or believe they have done all they can).

In early February the state board collates reports from the 96 local chapters and issues a "short list" of issues based on their assessment of what locals frequently ask for, and what, in the eyes of the state leadership, is feasible to do. This short list is mailed to each local chaper.

The third step occurs in late February and early March when local chapters discuss the short list in general membership meetings and in their local boards. The local boards report membership reactions back to the state. In early April the state board makes a final selection of issues, and recommends to the state convention a slate of issues for the program.

The last phase of the consensus-taking process is a state convention in mid-April. Delegates, usually about 300 elected by local chapters, debate the state board recommendations. The floor debates are preceded by caucuses organized by interested delegates usually to fight for inclusion of some item dropped by the state. Each of the typically 12 issues (four action and eight study issues) is debated and can be amended or dropped by floor vote.

Once adopted by the convention, the state initiates a number of measures to carry out the intent of the membership. On action issues this would include lobbying at the state capitol, a letter-writing campaign, or publication of League reports. On issues adopted for study, the state generates study packages for local Leagues, which are used for the basis of local chapter meetings and debates.

The large emphasis placed by the League upon consensus as opposed to some other criteria of selection such as majoritarian rule is intended to avoid schisms within the League as well as to include as many different viewpoints in the program. The League defines consensus as "agreement on broad objectives and general preferences, among a substantial number of members, representative of the membership as a whole, reached after sustained study and group discussion." The current state president suggests that even members who do not attend meetings and do not participate in consensus formation nevertheless believe in the process sufficiently to continue supporting League positions: "Consensus is not only what your membership agrees upon, but also that which your membership who didn't agree will let you do." Implicitly, arrival at consensus allows the leadership considerable discretion in carrying out the mandate of members.

DILEMMAS: OLIGARCHY AND THE GRASS ROOTS

Despite the historical commitment to internal democracy and the apparent openness of the program decision making, in fact, an unintended but almost inevitable tendency toward oligarchy or rule by a few occurs. The sources of this tendency are not difficult to perceive. The decision process is long, cumbersome, and expensive in terms of personal commitments of time and energy. This means that only the most zealous members and those holding elected office at state or local levels are capable of following the three-month process. The average member is distant from the decision and, except for the early discussions in January, plays little or no role in program selection. Instead, as local leaders expressed in interviews during the course of the research, a smaller group of state leaders and local board members who do most of the collating and summation of member views essentially determine the issues on the program.

We can assume, in the case of the League, that the withdrawal of membership interest is a voluntary decision by individuals who have other more compelling interests and activities. Yet a second source of oligarchy prevents even those who are actively interested in the decision from having much influence. That is, the entire process relies upon propagative communications technologies which are effective in handling vertical messages (from the state leadership to locals) but function poorly at handling communications among local chapters. Put another way, there are no horizontal communication links that allow active local members to communicate with similar persons in other locals.

The lack of such horizontal linkages means that local chapters that oppose certain issues advanced by the state leadership cannot get support for their opposition among other locals. Local delegates can attend the convention to form caucuses and lobby for changes, but by then it is often too late. A local president comments:

> Usually we go to convention with little preparation and if we object to the State's program try to caucus together. But with 300 women in a convention, only two days to organize, and few channels of communication at the convention to contact the 96 local leagues, notwithstanding that their delegates may go to other caucuses, there is little that one or two local chapters can do. When the issue comes to the floor you'll get killed by the State Board unless you have a number of locals backing a floor debate. It just never happens.

Hence even in an open convention composed of independently elected delegates, the proposals of the state leadership are ratified with little discussion or effective opposition.

It is conceivable that local chapters, which are spread across 300 miles from North to South, could use the mail to inform other locals of their opposition. In the past, however, this has not been done, largely due to the cost and time required to organize this kind of opposition. As one local president who had mounted such a campaign several years ago comments, the other local chapters "just file your letter in a waste basket as another piece of mail. It has no punch; they don't even know who you are, and they don't think it would work."

With the only effective means of organization-wide communication in the hands of the state leadership (a monthly publication, an offset press, and an automated general membership mailing list) the actual process of consensus-taking is a ritual creating the illusion of grass-roots democracy but does not indicate state control over the program to local chapters. The tendency toward oligarchy is visible in other areas of the League. Given the length of the consensus process, and the need for the state to take public stands on issues as they arise in the state legislature, the state boards on occasion will take a public position on issues that the local chapters have not specifically discussed. This occurred, for instance, in 1971 when the state opposed the dedication of gambling taxes to educational programs and supported a general income tax in the state legislature. The state argued these positions were consistent with previous consensus outcomes supporting a general income tax. Yet several locals and a large percentage of members objected to this interpretation. While the members had supported a general income tax, many in subsequent years had changed their minds and felt a new League position desirable. Others supported an income tax but did not oppose use of gambling funds for education. Briefly, the state board can exercise a great deal of discretion when implementing the program of the League. This process of implementation, in addition to selection of a program, is largely beyond the effective influence of the local chapters.

As in the larger society of which it is a part, members tend to trust their local chapter leaders more than state League leaders. In a survey of members, nearly a third of the members "wonder if state leaders listen to the average member." Even in an organization composed of independent local chapters, with a strong historical legacy of democracy, and one whose members are among the most educated and active in the society, the factors of size, time, and inequality in the means of political influence are sufficient to create an unintended oligarchy.

DESIGN OF A CITIZEN TECHNOLOGY

In our early discussions with the League, it became apparent to both the researchers and the state leadership that some sort of horizontal communications net linking up local Leagues before the convention might inhibit some of the tendency toward oligarchy described above. The prospect of providing a video television network linking the 96 locals was quickly discarded: a microwave system similar to the Metropolitican Regional Council television experiment described in Chaper 2 would cost several hundred thousand dollars and require two years to install. Equally disappointing in the early stages was our investigation of educational television in New Jersey. It was conceivable that, using a central studio broadcasting to the local chapter headquarters, and using telephone for the return message, we could provide something like an electronic town hall meeting. Unfortunately in one respect, at least, educational television is severely underdeveloped in New Jersey and is composed of two poor-quality UHF channels which cover only parts of the state. In another respect, it was fortuante we could not follow this route. The so-called electronic town hall idea had all the markings of a typical mass media call-in television show. Surely not all 96 local chapters would be able to speak; the experience would have been unsatisfying to many.

The only available technology that fit both the political requirements outlined in previous chapters and the economic criteria was telephone conferencing. Early estimates suggested a technology cost of around $2,000, depending on how it was used. Moreover, the New Jersey Bell system had a telephone conference "bridge" which was capable of connecting 30 telephones into a single circuit, using an operator to actually make the connections. Alternatively, three groups of ten each could be established on separate circuits.

The next question was, how could the technology be used? A conference call with 96 participants was impossible, given the technology. A conference call of even 30 persons seemed too large to permit easy give-and-take conversation.

The solution seemed to lie in the direction of staging conference calls composed of smaller groups of Leagues, say 10 or 12 participants in each call, each of whom would represent a single League. For instance, in a single night beginning at 7:30 p.m. a group of 30 local League presidents could have a conference call lasting one hour. They could be organized into small groups of ten each. In the following hour a different group of 30 could meet on the telephone circuits. The next evening, a different group of 30 would meet. In two nights it would be possible for all the 96 local presidetns to have met with other presidents. This "staging" process was selected to carry out the experiment.

The next question was, which president should meet with which presidents? Local presidents could be divided into groups of ten randomly, or, could be assigned on some principle of social distance. Originally, random assignment was thought desirable. State leaders quickly convinced us that it would be better to connect local Leagues on a regional basis. Local chapters in northern bedroom suburbs had more in common with other Leagues in their own region than with southern, rural Leagues. If one purpose of the calls was to produce common positions on League matters springing from shared concerns, a regional basis made more sense. Hence, local chapters were assigned to groups of 10 or 12 on this basis, and the groups remained the same throughout the experiment.

The last question was, when and how often should the meeting take place? As many of the local presidents were not acquainted with one another, much less with the technology, it seemed that one meeting was insufficient. Moreover, the structure of decision making argued for at least three different conference-call sessions: one after the local chapters had discussed the new program (late January), one after the state League had distributed its selection or "short list" (late February), and a final conference session to discuss the final state platform before the convention (late March). This schedule was adopted.

To summarize, then, each of the local League presidents would meet three times with other presidents in the region. The telephone meetings occurred in January, February, and March. In each conference call, an operator would dial a preselected list of numbers and connect groups of 10 to 12 presidents. It was decided to use home telephones, obviating the need for any travel on the part of the presidents.

DATA COLLECTION

One advantage of designing the experiment for a single large organization is that this strategy allows intensive data collection, sacrificing representativeness of a much broader design of, say, several organizations for much finer detailed information in a single setting.

Two concerns shaped our data collection. Foremost was the desire to understand the effects of this new sociotechnical system of telephone conferencing upon decision making and consensus formation in the League. We wanted to know how effective the new system was in creating greater interlocal agreement, increasing the influence of local Leagues over the League program, and thereby making the program more representative. A second concern was to measure the psychosocial dynamics involved in using the system. Would the inability to see other faces hinder communication, impede or expedite the flow of information, tone up or down the emotional content of debate? Would the rural Leagues who typically feel more left out of League politics accept the system less readily than the suburban northern chapters?

A battery of six different surveys was used to provide some quantitative answers to these questions. The most important surveys were a saturation survey of the entire membership, a panel survey of 17 randomly selected Leagues questioned before and after the experiment, and a three-wave panel survey of the local presidents completed after each conference call.

While quantitative data provide some overall estimate of the conference calls, important gaps remain on the more subtle effects of the calls. How is it possible to know what actually transpired on the conference circuits without a recording? We decided to record the last two conference sessions to provide this more intimate description. Transcripts of these calls, as it turned out, are much more effective than quantitative data in providing the reader with an understanding of the results.

Hence in the analysis below we frequently use these transcripts to substantiate our points, and use quantitative data to provide additional substantiation. Each of the participants was asked her opinion about recording of the calls, and where a single president objected, the calls were not recorded. Two groups were not recorded on this basis.

In addition to quantitative and transcript data, additional information was obtained through personal interviews and documents.

In the end, the League was among the most thoroughly investigated organizations in social science annals. The openness, forbearance, and concern of the members and their leaders contributed in large part to the success of our evaluation effort.

AN OVERVIEW

A partial answer to the question of how well the conference calls worked can be obtained by briefly reviewing the results from the presidents' surveys which occurred after each call. One measure tabulated how much agreement or consensus existed among the presidents both before and after the experiment (Figure 2). On this objective measure (based on individual presidents' ranking

FIGURE 2

Convergence over Time in the League

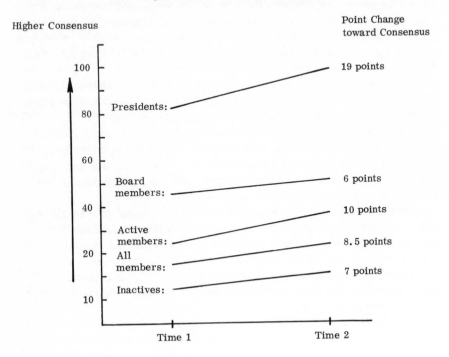

Source: Compiled by the author.

the program issues in order of importance) it can be seen that the local presidents who used the conference calls moved roughly twice as far toward consensus as relevant control groups. A part of this change is due to greater activism and involvement of presidents, but only half of the change comes from this source, and the remaining is due to the conference-call participation. This despite the fact that presidents were higher in consensus to begin with.

Other survey data on local president attitudes support this finding. Sixty percent of the conference participants felt that a consensus on League priorities had been attained by the third call. The ability to reach agreement and form coalitions depends in part on how easily people can fully discuss and react to debate on issues. Eight percent of the local presidents said they had a chance to express their views during the calls; 68 percent reported that access to the discussion was easy, and 65 percent said they were able to join the discussion whenever desired. Only 7 percent of the participants said the discussion was harder to join than a face-to-face discussion, and only 3 percent said they found it harder to perceive others' opinions than in face-to-face meetings.

These findings partially support the conclusion that the electronic conference calls were, on both objective and subjective grounds, sufficient to encourage agreement and coalition formation. The conference calls were no less effective than face-to-face meetings by and large. The advantage of the conference calls is that where face-to-face meetings are impossible, existing technology can provide a functional alternative.

A second question concerns the political consequences of the new system. After the third call many of the participants believed that the greater knowledge and consensus achieved among the local branches would affect the political balance at the convention in April. Forty-three percent of the presidents said the calls would facilitate formation of caucuses at the convention; 46 percent said the calls would increase the representativeness of the convention vote.

A better idea of the actual effect of the calls on the convention in April comes from an analysis of the survey conducted on all 195 convention delegates. Fifty-one of these were presidents (who thus participated in the calls), and 244 other delegates were elected by their locals. Thirty-five percent of the presidents at convention said participation in the calls changed their votes on the state program (17 percent of the others), and 28 percent of the presidents at convention said other delegates had mentioned the calls as one influence on their vote.

Early in the experiment we worried over the social-psychological aspects of the technology: faces cannot be seen, participants do not initially know one another (let alone their voices), and the conversation we feared might be stilted and emotionally cold. These fears were largely groundless. Sixty-two percent of the presidents reported the calls intimate and friendly, 88 percent said the discussion flowed easily without interruptions, and 86 percent said the quality of participation was eager and direct. A little over one-half of the participants reported difficulty in identifying the speaker after the first call, but as members became more familiar with the technology and the other voices, this difficulty declined, according to 40 percent of the presidents after the third call.

A series of three questions sought to measure the overall acceptance of the technology by the presidents. Here it can be seen that the majority of the local presidents judged the calls a success and favored making them a regular feature of the League's decision-making process. Sixty percent assessed the calls as a "very effective way to conduct a dialogue on League issues," and 61 percent said they would like the League to use the conference calls on a regular basis. Over 75 percent observed that conference calling was "not just another gimmick, but a promising innovation."

CRITICAL ISSUES: A CLOSER VIEW

While survey information can provide a gross description of a social process very efficiently, it provided little feeling for how a social process actually works. Providing this kind of understanding is important in an exploratory study such as ours. For instance, most of the League program issues suggested by the state leadership were noncontroversial; a strong consensus usually existed on most issues, either to put it in the program or dispense with it. Three issues generated considerable controversy and came to dominate discussion on the conference-call circuits. Each of these issues became controversial in part as a result of the state leaders' exercise of discretion—its ability to drop from consideration even popular issues and the ability to change the meaning of program items in the process of implementation. Moreover, these issues are controversial because there are strong opposing points of view on either side. To see how the conference calls were influential in shaping the ultimate League program we shall follow these critical issues from conference-call discussion to ultimate convention vote, making use of the recorded conference-call transcripts. These same transcripts provide us in turn with a much finer understanding of the process of reaching agreement and coalition formation with the new technology.

Administration of Justice: A Successful Mobilization

In addition to its broad discretion over financial arrangements, the state board's most important discretionary role is its ability to influence the League's program. While it is constrained in some respects by its past history, ideals, and members, it nevertheless has a greater capacity to slant the program toward one or more projects than has any other group within the League. In specific cases this means the state board can determine just what specific items will be studied under a general program rubric such as fiscal reform; in other cases the state board can decide to drop from the initial program agenda certain very popular items and replace them with projects more to its liking, its sense of timing and importance, though clearly less popular. The following two cases illustrate how the local presidents responded to this use of discretionary state board power, and how the conference calls aided local leaders to oppose these decisions.

The most popular "new item" (a project that had not previously been studied or pursued) was a study of the administration of justice with special emphasis on the courts and prisons. Like other states, New Jersey had recently experienced a number of prison riots, indictments of state judiciary officials, and scandals in the state prison system, all of which heightened public attention on the system of justice.

Though the state board after the first round was aware of the popularity of this proposed project, supported by 32 local Leagues, it chose instead to place on the program a land-use study which was initially supported by only 25 Leagues.

The reasons given by the state board were several. It was pointed out to the members that the national organization had been studying land use for several years and had many materials available to local Leagues. Hence it was "easier" than a new study; moreover, several local chapters had engaged in small local studies. It was also the sense of the board that historically this was the right moment for a comprehensive New Jersey land-use plan to emerge, and the League could play an important and influential role in its development if it adopted a project study now:

> While it was quite clear that members wished to continue to act under our present items, it also became quite clear that they want a new study item on the 1973-75 State Program. Three areas of interest came out way ahead of all the many, many items proposed: Mass Transportation, System of Justice, (including the courts, law enforcement and our prison system) and Land Use.
>
> The Board carefully weighed each item against our Program choosing criteria and finally decided to propose Land Use as a new study item. The deciding factors were many, but the one which carried the most weight was that land use policy is a key to solving problems in many areas of League concern. Additionally, the exigencies of the situation in New Jersey demands a study of land use *now*. Tomorrow will be too late if the League is to have maximum impact into assuring that New Jersey has an environment beneficial to life and programs and policies which meet the economic and social needs of the citizens.

In interviews the state board agreed that administration of justice was an important area, but that only one new item could effectively be adopted, and land use was more appropriate.

Resistance to the state board's decision centered about two contiguous local chapters which also happened to be connected in the conference call circuits. The focus of resistance centered about the need for a totally new program item which would serve to generate interest among current members as well as attract new members. Transcripts from the two recorded conference calls reveal how the calls were useful in originating and coordinating the formation of a caucus at the state convention. In the transcripts that follow, individual presidents of local chapters are identified with a "P."

P: Well why don't we ask first whether, Myra, are you planning a caucus?

P: Yes. In fact I got together last night with Donna and our next president. We are planning a caucus. Let me apologize. The Linden League name was not in the list of the state supporting the administration of justice item. But we will be having a caucus, and we are planning to send out flyers to those Leagues who indicated on the nonrecommended items that they were interested in administration of justice. If there is anyone else who would like to receive a copy of the scope of the item as we have planned it, let me know. We want to get as much information to the interested League hands before the convention and then we will have the same type of flyer for League delegates at convention.

P: Yes, Donna, this is Judy, would you send us one?

P: Lydia A., West Orange. Would you send one? I think it would really, if you can afford it, be a good idea to send it to every League in the state.

P: Well, the only reason we came out against that is because I receive enough mail here, really, you get so many pieces of information in the mail, that I just file them away. And we couldn't afford it, but in any event we didn't feel just a mailed flyer would work, just broadcast out there. But you girls, would you all like one?

P: Yes.

P: Plainfield. We were only put down by state as supporting one non-recommended item, but there were many more we supported.

P: We were confused, too. This is Rosemary S. We went over the state list of Leagues supporting nonrecommended items; they had Providence down for things we had discussed but did not support. We got put down on five of them. We couldn't figure how the state made the list.

P: All you girls realize, of course, that in supporting administration of justice, that means we are against mass trasportation. That is, if one is going to be practical in taking home a workable program.

P: Right.

P: We can't have two new items.

P: Land use or mass transportation.

And from another conference call:

P: We found a tremendous interest on the second round in administration of justice. Are any of you going to be having a caucus at convention?

P: Someone is, but I don't know who. Someone is.

P: This is Betty L. From West Essex, and we suggested children's rights; but on second thought, we did feel that probably we could get together with the people of administration of justice, we could come in as part of it. If we could get together somehow and arrange to get children's rights, then we would go along with administration of justice.

P: We proposed a study of individual liberties, citizen rights, but that falls into administration of justice, too.

P: Right, if there is some interest, if we could get together at convention and, you know, see how far we could get with it.

P: It's a tremendous area, so broad.

P: Do any of you feel that the state board has acted arbitrarily in pulling one new item out of the recommended items?

P: No, I think that's their prerogative. That is what they should do, give that kind of direction.

P: If we don't like it, we could change it.

P: And I think in caucuses we can do that.

P: I was just asking why do they just want one item? When it is up to the League to decide if they want one new item?

P: Well, that's what you're going to vote on at convention. You have that opportunity.

P: I understand that, but why should they recommend only one item?

Several points deserve emphasis. First the calls were apparently seen as more effective than the traditional mail-out flyer sent to all local chapters for coordinating resistance to the state. As most local presidents receive a great deal of mail, it was felt such a broadcast technique would not result in people's taking the notion of a new study item seriously. Second, it is too expensive to mail out flyers in most Leagues. The conference calls also seem more flexible, allowing the message to be custom-fitted to the audience. Thus when questions arose about just what the item included, a proponent was able to say immediately that it did not include a study of police but focused more on the judiciary and prison systems. This kind of flexibility usually cannot be foreseen in a mailed flyer.

In the conference calls, the proponents of administration of justice were forced to restrict and specify the scope of their study in light of objections that the program was becoming too large. Most presidents seemed to feel the state could afford to study only one new item, most likely land use. To this objection the proponents responded that land use was not really a new item, that it had been studied before, and that a new item could and should be mounted to attract new members. This kind of specification and rationale no doubt could have been developed in a face-to-face caucus meeting at convention, but by then it may well have been too late; as it turned out, the proponents arrived at convention with a concise description of the study they planned, and well-tested rationales for why it should be adopted.

Resolution: Consensus Formation

The vote on the administration of justice item provided the only real drama of the convention.

The most prominent counterargument was that the program was already too large. On the first vote, the item lost with only 231 supporting votes, just 7 votes short of the required two-thirds necessary to place an item on the program from the floor. A roar of protest rose up from convention floor supporters that the issue required debate and argument, to which the leadership acceded.

The supporters of administration of justice, in their speech, appealed to those delegates who voted for a study of children's rights, and essentially bargained with them by broadening the study of administration of justice to include a study of the juvenile justice system as well. This tactic worked, as the final vote produced 281 supporters, enough for passage.

Resistance to State Leader Mobilization: Tax Dedication

The discretionary role of the state board in determining the League's program is uniquely illustrated by its ability to recall issues that the League had supported in the past and to lobby for their inclusion a new program. In February 1973, the state board sent a flyer to all local chapters seeking approval on the new program of a controversial issue that the League had supported weakly up until 1967, namely, opposition to the dedication of taxes. This position was intended by the leadership to be included under the general rubric of fiscal responsibility and to support the League's past and current efforts to legislate a state income tax.

Revenue collected for the exclusive use of a particular service or function of government is called dedicated. In some cases the source and beneficiary are closely connected, as in the case of fuel taxes supporting highway construction and repair. In other cases, such as state lottery support for education, the connection is distant. In any case, the principal consequence of dedication from the point of view of public management is that the activity so funded is removed from legislative control.

Dedication is not specifically prohibited by the New Jersey constitution of 1844, still in effect up to 1948. By 1930 there were 30 special funds; by 1932 dedicated funds accounted for three-fourths of all the money spent by state government. Only one-fourth of the state budget, in other words, was susceptible to democratic or legislative control. Constitutional reforms of 1944 and 1948 avoided the tax-dedication issue by compromising on a single appropriation law and the creation of a single state fund. However, this left unclear precisely how money was collected and how it would be used; the result is that the legislature still passes dedicated funds, and the matter of constitutionality has never been litigated. In general, farm groups and highway construction and use groups such as truckers supported tax dedication; the beneficiaries of such a system seem to outweigh the political clout of those who pay taxes.

Good government groups of one sort or other have always opposed dedicated taxes. In times of depression, highways are being built out of burgeoning highway funds, while simultaneously schools are crumbling and health services are nonexistent. The League flyer distributed in February 1973 outlined the League's opposition:

1. Dedication hampers sound fiscal management. The yield of a given tax will seldom match the purpose for which it is dedicated. If the yield is too large, extravagance is encouraged; if too small, a needed service is curtailed. Since needs change and the tax yields fluctuate, there is little chance that they will change in the same proportion over the years.
2. It makes for inflexibility of the revenue system, with the consequence that legislatures experience difficulty in matching revenues to priorities.
3. "Earmarking" infringes on the policy-making powers of the executive and legislature, since it removes a portion of governmental activities from periodic review and control.
4. Once dedication is allowed, pressures increase from lobbying and special interest groups to dedicate a tax for their "pet" program.

Opponents believe that legislature can most effectively carry out its responsibility of efficient use of public funds by careful review of all revenue sources, establishment of state priorities and measures to assure sound management practices by all departments of state government. This can best be accomplished without the straitjacket effect that a series of dedicated funds would impose.

The historical position of the League on dedication is somewhat ambivalent, reflecting the fact that it has caused a great deal of controversy within the League. While the League has supported a single state fund and budget since 1945, a statement opposing dedication of taxes was defeated in the 1955-57 program; later, in 1957-59, this statement was approved. In 1961 the League adopted support for a graduated income tax as its major fiscal responsibility item; clearly, opposition to dedication had become secondary. Finally, in 1967, the item was dropped entirely.

The League's support for a graduated income tax, as opposed to the existing regressive sales tax, met with near success when in 1964 the state assembly passed the income tax, but it was reversed in the senate by one vote. The election of a reform Democratic governor in 1972, a silent preelection supporter of income taxes, reinvigorated New Jersey's reform groups, and clearly the League was desirous of playing a role in ensuring passage of tax reform legislation. Unfortunately, when the vote came in July 1974, the assembly passed by one vote an income tax, but it never came to the senate because of defections from Democratic party ranks.

In any event, the state board recognized that opposition to dedication of taxes was an important part of its support for an income tax and sought member approval of this plank for the 1973-74 program. The general membership and local leaders had decidedly different views.

While the League has generally supported the notion of graduated income taxes, it has been a very unpopular position within the League. In the words of one president, "We intellectually support the notion but when we go back home and talk to the husband and neighbors we don't dare speak up." The ambivalence in the League is attributable to the fact that most members come from wealthy communities where property taxes are enormously high, indeed, the highest in the nation. However, it seems to be the feeling in wealthy suburbs that if an income tax were passed, property taxes would remain the same, and income taxes would simply add to the overall tax burden. While the reformers argue that most people would experience a decline in local property taxes as local schools and other services would switch to state funding, the governor's own data suggest wealthy persons would actually pay slightly more taxes. Local real estate agents, strong opponents of income taxes, argue that the wealthy communities will never let their schools deteriorate to the average state funding level, and hence property taxes will certainly not fall.

The ambivalence toward the dedication item appears related to the ambivalence toward tax reform. Dedicated taxes offer one way out of the dilemma: by creating specialized funds like a state lottery, off-track betting parlors, and other forms of popular legalized gambling, no income tax would be needed. The success of the 1970 state lottery in New Jersey only encouraged such beliefs. Other forms of legalized gambling are now actively being debated.

But opposition to the state's position on the dedication of taxes had other bases as well, principally centered about the feeling that the state was not following any consensus of the membership, as the following transcripts reveal:

P: Perhaps because so many members are new and were not in the League when we studied dedication of taxes, it might be worthwhile to make one of the very early meetings next year, and instead of putting dedication of taxes in the wording of the program to take a consensus and reaffirm that that's where our members do stand. It seems to me if we're going to be against dedicated taxes it would be better to have our members go through the consensus process so that they really understand what we're against.

P: That's a very valid point. It's been assumed that the consensus has been taken.

P: And then the wording was changed on the tax item. Course in the old days of the League you couldn't bring a position back.

P: When did that change?

P: I thought that was the policy too?

P: No, somehow, I don't know how it had changed, but in the '67 tax item, opposition to dedication of taxes was not in the wording of the item, only the proposal for income taxes. Now the state realizes opposition to dedication of taxes should have been in the item, so they want to bring it back as a position.

P: You see the thing that's at stake here is a League principle that we have in the past few years been skipping over, and maybe it's alright. The idea is that you don't study something once it's been dropped and you want to put it back on, you just put the wording on. Or, in the case of housing, when they put that under the Human Resources item at the national level, we didn't study it; they just assumed we wanted to support it. And I'm sure that's true.

P: It sort of goes against the old League objective of member control.

P: That's right, and the thing is, this sort of thing starts out being just fine, and then pretty soon the state board is putting on whatever it thinks the League should agree to. It could deteriorate to that. I don't think necessarily it would.

P: I think the point being made is League procedure rather than the particular item. Isn't that what you're saying?

P: Yes, that's what I'm saying. It's the procedure.

P: That tends to lead us to a whole different thing. Do we want to be careful, or do we want to let state know that we want to be careful about maintaining procedures that the League has had? Because, of course, bringing it to the consensus, then going back to the state board is necessarily slower, and in these days when you want to take action quickly, does the League really want to continue its style for which it's noted, a very slow style? I think it's a philosophy of the League question we're discussing.

From another conference call, the extent to which the state board's position was taken without the membership's awareness becomes more clear:

P: Do most of your Leagues support this opposition to dedicated taxes?
P: No.
P: We've never discussed it, I was never even aware that we had a position like this. I've only been involved in the League since '68 in Jersey. I don't even remember having discussed it before.

These remarks reveal some well known, yet interesting facets of consensus-building in an organization such as the League. Even in an organization devoted to the fulfillment of democracy, it is necessary for the leadership to act quickly and in certain instances without a clear-cut support from membership; in the case of tax dedication, the leadership felt this was in important issue which the League could take effective action on in the upcoming year, given a reform governor and a Democratic majority in both houses. Hence the desire to quickly reinstate opposition to dedicated taxes as a part of the League package.

Second, the traditional consensus mechanisms of the League are slow and inefficient relative to the demands for quick action. Even to readopt an old issue means educating the new members, discussing the issue in 96 local chapters, and devoting an entire meeting to debate; finally, the issue has to be readopted by vote of the convention delegates, who meet only once in two years.

Third, in the absence of relatively efficient consensus mechanisms, the state leadership fills a kind of vacuum by trying to update League positions as legislative and political opportunities for effective action arise. And this pressure to act leads, as in the case of tax dedication, and despite commitment to democratic ideals, to adoption of positions not approved by the members, pressure tactics by the state to obtain support without debate, and the use of deliberately vague phrasing of positions to allow the leadership maximum flexibility and give credence to the claim of acting under a broad mandate.

These problems, and our analysis, are hardly new. They reflect the traditional dilemma of very large representative political structures in which the need for executive action comes up against the historical commitment to and need for popular support. The resolution of this dilemma is typically to afford the executive great license to act under a general mandate, and to hold him accountable infrequently. That such a resolution leads to the emergence of oligarchs and to the growth of popular cynicism and alienation requires no repetition here. The question, however, is whether this reflects an iron law of oligarchy to which all large representative structures are inescapably doomed, or rather does it reflect a failure to develop more efficient consensus mechanisms? We shall return to this question in the concluding chapter.

Resolution of Tax Dedication

The precise contribution of the conference calls to the final outcome on the tax dedication issue is difficult for us to trace. There was no specific caucus arranged to oppose the state board's position. From our conference call transcripts we do know that the calls helped spread the word among presidents that many Leagues no longer opposed dedication of taxes; we do know from interviews with local presidents and from local documents that several Leagues protested the state board's position in letters sent to state headquarters. However, in the end vote, the state position was carried at convention by a vote of 290 for, 60 opposed, without any debate.

Centralization of National League Finances

One of the more controversial issues faced by the League during 1973 was one not even on the proposed state program and not known even to our research team until the controversy erupted over the conference circuits. The focus of this debate was the 1972 national League decision that mandated that every local chapter must submit four dollars for each member directly to the national League without going through state League coffers. The state

Leagues were still obligated to pay a "fair share" of state proceeds to the national. In the case of New Jersey, this "fair share" amounted to $24,000.

The 1972 national League resolution on finances was opposed by New Jersey and several other states, but was carried by a narrow margin. Its intended effect, according to the national chairman at the time, was to strengthen the League into a powerful national lobby for women and progressive government in general. In consequence, by circumventing the state Leagues altogether and going directly to the locals, the new financial arrangements considerably weakened the state Leagues. Moreover, as several local presidents argued, it would impair the grass-roots strength of locals by draining funds from local projects to large but equally distant national programs. In short, the new arrangements threatened to change the League from a grass-roots organization to just another Common Cause-type lobby.

The reaction of the New Jersey state League was to withhold one-third of its "fair share" contribution ($8,000) in 1973, thereby maintaining the same level of funding from New Jersey to the national as obtained in 1972. The result was that the national obtained its local pledges from the local chapters, but lost an equal amount from the state's pledge. (See Chapter 3 for the history of this issue.)

The decision of the state board to withhold financial support from the national League was taken unilaterally by the state without a formal consensus, vote, or lobbying effort to the local chapters. In our early interviews with the League the topic never arose with League officials, and hence the investigators were unaware that a controversy even existed. For this reason we have very little survey data concerning membership attitudes on this issue. By the time of the state convention the issue had surfaced into a controversy, and we do have data on convention delegates that can be of some help.

Opposition to the state League's unilateral decision to cut back support to the national came largely from one local and its president. Ridgewood, a large, prosperous League, had sent several letters to the state League protesting the action. Rather early in the controversy, Mrs. Linden, president of the Ridgewood local, recognized that the only hope of changing the state policy was through a floor vote at the convention in April 1973. This would require a mail lobbying effort of other locals before the convention to stimulate support and force into the open any opposition. A pamphlet was sent to all locals seeking to restore a least $4,000 to the national:

SUPPORT FOR NATIONAL
THE MAIN ISSUE   To be an effective organization the League must operate well at all levels. We are one organization, depending on one another. Each level of the League gains strength from what the other can do best.

The fundamental financial base of the League is the local Leagues. It is up to us to support all levels of League. Both state and national depend upon local League support.

THE CURRENT PROBLEM   National, in carrying out what local Leagues have asked it to do and what it is uniquely situated to do, is suffering a major financial shortage.

Already national has proposed cutbacks for the coming year.
1. Reduced publications.
2. Fewer field visits to state and local Leagues.
3. Reduced operations in HR and EQ to make way for Land Use.
4. Continuing one less board meeting, one less Voter.
5. Not filling staff vacancy in PR until mid-year at least.
6. Fewer national committee meetings and fewer members on committees.

The proposed national budget is based on states' meeting their fair shares and further cuts will be necessary if states do not approach them.

NEW JERSEY PLEDGE   New Jersey has pledged 2/3 of the amount requested by national. Last year, New Jersey pledged $10,000 and increased that amount to $15,000 during the year when our picture became clearer under the new financial arrangement. State recommends raising this year's pledge by $747. This leaves New Jersey $8,000 short of its fair share.

NEW JERSEY CAN DO BETTER   Perhaps it is unrealistic to expect to reach the full amount, but surely we can do better than 2/3. New Jersey is in a good financial position. The state League has given excellent services to local Leagues, managing still to have some excess receipts at the end of the year. In fact, our total reserves increased from $30,024 to $33,642.

SUPPORT FOR NATIONAL AT A GLANCE
NATIONAL NEEDS SUPPORT

Last year (1972-73):

$23,692	Amount requested by national
$15,000	Amount New Jersey gave, roughly 2/3 of request

This coming year (1973-74):

$23,692	Amount requested by national
$15,747	Amount proposed in New Jersey budget, roughly 2/3 of request

NEW JERSEY RESERVES

$24,000	Minimum level recommended by handbook for operating budget of $96,000.
$30,000	Level the state boards regards as sufficient.
$33,642	Actual reserve at year end, March 31, 1973.

2/3 of our fair share is not enough.
NATIONAL NEEDS IT. NEW JERSEY CAN PROVIDE IT.

The pamphlet and postage were relatively inexpensive but required 20 man-hours to complete and address; this is one of the traditional ways in which a local League with sufficient resources and commitment can attempt to influence other local Leagues and the state board. Moreover the costs of a pamphlet sent to the entire membership would be prohibitive. Only the state organization, which controls the membership address file, has sufficient resources for this kind of internal organization lobbying. In point of fact, few Leagues have resources for a limited mailing to 96 local chapters, and therefore it is not commonly done. In any event, the conference calls entered the lobbying effort as a forum for direct expression of opposition, compromise proposals, and finally seeking others' commitments to attend a caucus at convention. The transcript from the third and final conference call in Mrs. Linden's group illustrates how the calls could be used to mobilize support for opposition to the state. In the transcripts that follow, Mrs. Linden is identified with an "L".

L: June, at some point after we finish discussing program I would like to bring up another area which I have written to all of you about, which would be Ridgewood's position on the budget.

P: I was just going to ask you that [laughter] ; why don't you do it now?

L: Okay. Maybe the best thing would be to summarize our position and then get into it. I think everybody received our letter but I'm not sure that everybody is clear. I sent it to every local League president, and the state board, so the state knows our position. Basically, it has to do with the state support to national, and it goes like this: in December when the state budget committee drew up the first state budget they proposed to support national $24,000, to be paid for by the income coming in from our pledges, other income, and use of $5,000 from reserves. But when the pledges came back they were lower than hoped, so when they revised the budget they decided to use only $1,000 from reserves instead of $5,000. The major change in the expenditure size was a reduction in the support to national from $24,000 to $16,000, or two-thirds of the national request. Now the Ridgewood League feels that their original plan to use the $5,000 was quite reasonable; and what we would like to see is that they put this back into the budget, not change the rest of the budget, but add to the national pledge the $4,000 which they have not taken out. Put use of reserves back into the budget, and increase the national pledge to $20,000. We've talked to a number of Leagues and found it very hard for the local Leagues to get a handle on the whole subject because it gets rather complex. You get into state and national budgets and use of funds, and reserves, and so forth. I've really come to the conclusion that we need more than ever to have some discussion about it because the local Leagues find it difficult to get enough information to make a good judgment; so what we would like to urge now is that people come to a meeting at the convention and discuss the whole area of the state pledge to national and what it means, and what reserves, and whatever other questions there are; and what I'd like to ask you now is whether you have any questions which maybe we could work on and get information on so that at a meeting at convention we could have a better discussion, more information to go on.

P: The question of state reserves, what are they? Our reserves are zero in Pascack valley.

L: I can say briefly. They are reserves at the present time of about $30,000. They get this from the fiftieth anniversary, special projects, and from operating surpluses. They have to get in more than they can spend. In the by-laws they need to have three months' operating expenses. This would be $24,000 according to the present budget of $96,000, so they would need about $24,000 to be sure they could pay off any obligations. The history of the local Leagues in paying pledges has been extremely good. So that the League is very sure of getting this income from the local Leagues. So they are in pretty good shape in paying their own obligations.

P: So why don't they want to pay some reserves to national?

L: I'm not sure. There was a difference in opinion on the board, apparently; you would have to go to a member of the state board to find out. We've had a lot of discussion about financing, and state and local, and about what we were getting back from them both, and every time I think it's very difficult to talk about over the phone, but I'll try. The national needs support in order for us to get the information that they pass out like on land use, committee guides. If we don't support them, what they will cut back is the services that we need rather than the things they spend tax-deductible education money on.

P: I think they spend money on things we don't need.

P: I think that's true, too.

P: Well for one thing I know they (national) just gave a cocktail party on election day, and that's one thing they could stop.

P: But we did that at the local once, and that can bring back lots of money, too. [laughter]

P: How has this been done historically?

L: For years we have fully supported national completely, I believe this is the first year we haven't.

P: How many were at national convention?

P: I was.

P: Well we were very disenchanted with national budget. I think this is still a residual reaction to that national meeting.

L: Our feeling, is that we might be cutting off our noses to spite our faces, we have some disagreements with national too, but we don't feel that keeping the funds down is going to be the way to solve them.

P: This is June L. again, Pascack Valley. On the discussion of local contributions. State should help locals raise money from local concerns.

L: We have reserved a room at convention for a caucus, and I would think the whole financial area could be covered at the caucus. We don't know the room number yet, so look for us.

P: We should explore more of this corporate contributions. Maybe we could get together in a corner of the caucus room and become acquainted.

P: How about local banks?

P: Well, our banks won't give a dime.

P: We got $100 from a local branch.

P: This is June L. again. I was never involved in finances until they made me finance chairman. I've had to rethink my thoughts on it since in my area all these national headquarters have moved in. We're considered a wealthy League, but lose members when we raise dues. I would hope that at your caucus you consider ways to get state to look at different ways of financing its obligations. The members just can't pay everything; I think there's more money out there in those corporations, and without state support the local Leagues just can't get it. They could get it. We can't get five for a little local League.

L: They certainly are related issues, and ah, will we see you at convention?

P: Yes.

L: Good, then we will bring up the possible alternative ways instead of going into reserves to get this money to the national. Who else will be at convention?

Several things emerged from this conversation and our subsequent interview with Mrs. Linden. First, it appeared during her conference calls that there was still significant reaction to the national League's attempt to increase contributions from local chapters, a move bitterly resisted by New Jersey Leagues. Second, use of state reserves to pay the national was not popular. A third potential source of compromise was to try other methods of raising new funds with which to support national, so-called easy money, like contacting local banks and businesses for contributions instead of expensive and time-consuming mail-out campaigns or garage sales. Thus what Mrs. Linden had thought might be a caucus limited to the issue of support to the national became a caucus that reviewed fund-raising activities by the state League. The caucus thus attracted many persons interested in state finances, who in turn might be convinced to support Ridgewood. However, the extent of opposition to the Ridgewood proposal for full support to the national League was very broad. Transcripts of other conference calls reveal that among local presidents the national organization was seen as the enemy of grass-roots activism as the following quotes indicate:

P: It seems at national we've increased the paid staff in the last years greatly. They can turn out a lot of material, send it down to the local level. They forget the locals don't have any paid staff.

P: Amen.

P: I really strongly object to what the national has done to the local Leagues. I know we're part of the national and we have to support it, but we always had been a grass-roots organization from the bottom to the top.

P: Right.

P: And in the past few years the national has initiated an eleborate program. I understand nearly all the fiftieth anniversary money is gone. And really they're such complex things that the locals, the delegates, really don't understand what the national is talking about. When they brought out that full load last, that $4 membership levy, we'd already had notices in our bulletin of our budget and so forth. It seems to me what they are doing in the day of the liberated women, and the women going back to work, what they're doing to League women, is pushing us back. Now we are holding garage sales and cooking dinner to make money to pay dues. The old idea was the League was some place where you kept the refreshments simple because you wanted to do something, and do we exist, at the local level, just to feed national?

Resolution of the Support for National Issue

While the conference calls were very useful to the Ridgewood League for contacting other presidents directly and urging their support, the calls also were obviously useful to those who opposed increased support to national. At convention, the National Support Caucus met under Mrs. Linden's guidance. Approximately 40 delegates were in attendance. After speeches from the convention floor, a vote was taken and the opposition plank passed in favor of full support to the national League. However, the state leadership called for a quorum count and found it lacking. In a few minutes delegates were pressed to return, and the measure lost by six votes.

In a subsequent interview, Mrs. Linden commented that without the conference calls it was unlikely her letter would have had as much effect:

> You just don't get the chance before convention to talk directly to 10 or 12 other presidents and make your case. By the time they come to convention it is too late. Either they never thought of the issue, or they think you are all alone. Even though we lost I was very happy. We never expected to come so close, with the support we got. Caucuses usually fail in getting their planks adopted by large margins so we were pleased to have done so well on a touchy issue.

Even though Mrs. Linden's mobilizing effort ultimately failed, it would appear that compared to the experience of previous caucuses her proposal did far better than expected; and that in part this was due to the influence of the conference calls in directly informing other local presidents and delegates of the issue as well as planning the caucus.

OVERALL EFFECT ON ORGANIZATIONAL OUTCOMES

The final program adopted by the state convention was the result of several factors: prior historical commitments, perceptions of state and local officials, and popular member support for certain issues. It is impossible to judge precisely the impact of our telephone conference calls upon these traditional factors or upon the final outcome. Forsaking precision momentarily, we did leave the Leauge with the sense of having tilted the political competition between the state leadership and the local chapters in favor of the latter.

Reviewing the success criteria outlined at the beginning of this chapter, it seems clear that the conference calls did indeed provide a new forum where common views and political coalitions could develop. In particular, this occurred with the highly controversial issues. Moreover, the new electronic forum was not a simply replacement for equally useful nonelectronic devices of influence such as letter writing. In fact, the conference calls seemed to reinforce the impact of these traditional tools: the calls helped bring people to convention caucuses, reminded people of a letter sent to all League presidents, and refreshed memories of past attempts at influence. This add-on feature has important consequences for maintaining checks and balances, which will be discussed below.

Second, the conference calls did have noticeable, albeit short-term political effects. No part of the state's program was dropped at convention, but sizeable opposition developed to its tax proposal, and a new issue which it had dropped (administration of justice) was forced by convention delegates upon the state League. As this has not happened before in recent League history, it seems safe to conclude that these were results of the conference calls. Listening to the transcripts only reinforces this conclusion.

Use of the conference calls did not present problems of either cost or skills to the League. The cost of the technology was less than $1,500 or about 1.5 percent of the League's annual budget. Although we had feared that the call participants would feel socially distant from one another, the biggest problem with the technology turned out to be integrity of the AT&T circuits. Roughly 30 percent of the local presidents reported that at one time or another in the three calls they had experienced technical difficulties. The typical technical problem was an inability to hear one or more parties to the conversation, and a fading in and out of participants.

Unfortunately, the costs could be a great deal less expensive with a more aggressive marketing policy on the part of AT&T, the parent company, and small technological improvements. AT&T purposely does not advertise the availability of conference call circuits, and, with the exception of high government officials and corporate executives, the circuits are rarely used. AT&T claims they lose money on conference calls because of the labor costs involved (operators have to dial participants manually) and high unit costs resulting from poor utilization of existing capital equipment. The result is that in New Jersey there is one conference-call "bridge" that allows a maximum number of 30 simultaneous participants (they can be organized as in our experiment, however, into various subgroups, such as three groups of ten participants or six subgroups of five participants each). Our experiment was forced to work with a technology nearly as old as the telephone, and this put definite limits on what we were able to accomplish. Although we went into the field hoping to involve all the membership of a large organization in the use of a new technology, actually we were forced to restrict ourselves to involving directly only the leaders of existing grassroots groups, and to rely on traditional feedback mechanisms such as reports and face-to-face encounters to inform the larger membership of the results of the conference calls. This mixture of the traditional with the innovative does have important beneficial implications, which will be discussed later.

An important cost reduction in conference calling occurred with the introduction of ESS circuits in many areas of the United States. This system totally automates through computer switching devices the process of making a phone call; more important, in these ESS regions small conference calls of up to four persons can be dialed directly from a customer's home phone. The cost of these calls is one-tenth that of manually connected calls. Unfortunately, only four persons can be connected, too few for our purposes, which would require a capability of at least ten persons.

Even in the ESS regions, AT&T does not aggressively market the new conference potential. Again cost considerations are cited by company executives.

A more immediate technological possibility for conference calls would be computer sweepout conference calls. In this system, customers wishing a conference circuit would submit to the telephone company lists of participants and their phone numbers in advance of the conference call. These lists would be punched on cards and fed into a central switching computer, which in turn would automatically dial and connect the individual phones by "sweeping out" from a central location.

Yet instead of developing these relatively simply innovations, which would rely mostly upon existing capital investment, AT&T has poured millions of dollars into a space-age gimmick called "picture phones." A large research and development program of the early 1960s led to the development of several model picture phones and their installation in certain high load areas. Yet their high cost and limited advantages over ordinary voice telephone circuits led customers to reject their permanent installation. Subsequent market studies by AT&T only confirmed the judgment of early users. The project was still being funded at a lower level as of 1974, with new elaborations (such as group picturephone conference rooms connecting major cities and rented to corporations) being developed.

One clear-cut finding of our research is that the much simpler voice-only conference call is entirely adequate to the discussion of most issues in a group setting. Moreover, the extension of this technology can proceed immediately without waiting for the year 2000. The technology is readily usable by virtually all citizens: no special connections or procedures are required, with their attendant high costs. Improvement of the existing technology, already accomplished in the ESS systems to some extent, appears likely to lead to a reduction in costs to one-tenth of the current rate. This potentially would allow a 10,000-member organization to use the conference networks at a cost of 1.5 cents a member. Greater utilization would in turn reduce unit costs, promising even further cost reductions, especially if the utilization occurred in nonpeak load periods (in the evening or Sunday morning, for instance).

One important criterion for evaluating the effects of citizen technology remains to be discussed: Can the technology be designed so as to preserve existing checks and balances?

PRESERVATION OF CHECKS AND BALANCES: THE "ADD-ON" FEATURE

All democratic organizations and societies develop formal and informal mechanisms to limit the ability of one leader or a small number of groups to gain control over all important political resources and positions. The formal division of power into executive, legislative, and judicial functions, and as well as customary yet informal arrangements which preserve autonomous, private universities, political parties, and other private associations, are examples of the kinds of checks and balances built into most democratic societies and organizations. They are to some lesser extent found as well even in so-called totalitarian nations. Their function is to limit authority by dividing it, to slow down the decision-making process by allowing diverse interests to veto or modify a policy and to protect critical cultural values from a tyrannical majority by structurally isolating those units designed to protect and preserve these values.

The emergence of mass-communications techniques, from muckraking newspapers to radio in the 1920s, later to color television and cable TV, are often seen as threats to the preservation of check and balance systems. In part, this is due to the very nature of their development as propagation devices discussed in Chapter 1. But fear of mass communications is more directly due to their use by totalitarian regimes since 1930: potentially the advances in telecommunications allow direct appeal to a mass audience by circumventing the layers of protective institutions. In such a manner formal and informal divisions of authority, which are limitations on executive power, can and have been overcome through plebiscitarian appeals made possible by modern technologies.

In our research we have illustrated that it is possible to consciously design new telecommunications tools that preserve existing checks and balances. The avoidance of plebiscitarianism is possible if two features are carefully pursued: first, restricting the scope of innovations to that of add-on features to existing institutions; and second, the use of interactive communication techniques that allow the participants to both send and receive messages rather than play the more passive audience role inherent in mass communications.

The add-on feature deserves further elaboration. In the League experiment there are several checks on popular sentiment: local leaders are elected for regular periods, and they can be removed only for violating the national and state charter; the state board, also elected at regular intervals, interprets the state charter to local Leagues; the state charter in turn must conform to the national League constitution; policy decisions of the state board must be approved by a state convention composed of member delegates. An important feature of our experiment is that none of these formal checks and institutional balances were disturbed. Rather the conference network provided a useful add-on to an existing structure permitting greater discussion of issues and the emergence of local subgroup coalitions. In such a manner plebiscitarian effects can be avoided. Unfortunately, in many current experiments and suggestions for use of new technologies in political decision making these strictures are not observed. Rather than enhancing the horizontal linkages between citizens and subgroups, many experimenters have uncritically sought to strengthen the already strong vertical linkages between elites and citizens.

ARTICULATION WITH THE POLITICAL PROCESS

Just as important in the development of new citizen technologies is the principle that they be closely articultated with an ongoing, real decision-making process. More simply, the new technologies should have a visible impact on how decisions are reached (the process) and on the ultimate collective decision (the results). Without this, the new technologies are merely gimmicks from the transistor grab bag. Worse, they masquerade as what they are not, heightening expectations, but ultimately adding to cynicism.

While most of the experiments in citizen technology are poorly articulated with decision-making structures, the current attempts of the mass media to build in so-called feedback from readers and listerners deserve special criticism. Whether in the form of on-the-street interviews, call-in radio and television shows, studio collections of "average citizens," opposition editorials in newspapers and on television, they suffer universally from the same fault: the feedback is in no way connected to real decisions or the process of decision making. These devices habitually recruit either the loudest or most outrageous opinions, always balanced by an overselection of "respectable" opinion in the hope it is more likely to be read and believed. They do not encourage the growth and maturation of diverse views but rather present "hard" positions. While providing a palliative to outraged groups and individuals who otherwise feel disconnected from the events that surround them, they just as surely maintain the perception of participants that this kind of feedback is of little use. Indeed, it is not, except in the sense that these programs are designed to illustrate that the mass-media institutions are concerned about what their viewers and readers think. Obviously it sells.

Yet in practice it is difficult to draw a sensible line between strengthening the articulation between citizen preferences and collective decision making without destroying or weakening beneficial checks and balances in a democratic polity. A long-recognized informal balance in most democratic polities is the ignorance, apathy, and powerlessness of a large percentage of the adult population. Presumably this inhibits the emergence of a passionate, tyrannical majority and grants to political executives a wider latitude of action than formally accorded. This balance mechnism no doubt will be disturbed by the development of citizen technologies along the lines suggested here.

In the earliest designs of our experiment, we had hoped to use a very large conference-call network involving all members, to arrive at a decision binding on the organization. This possibility was never broached to the League. The lack of technology was one factor in the decision, but it also appeared too risky from the organization's point of view to place much trust in something called a Conference Call Convention as a replacement for the traditional convention used in the previous 50 years. While a Conference Call Convention might have proved beyond a doubt that new technologies can aid democratic organizations, it could also have been an unmitigated disaster. A more conservative approach was adopted where the technology would simply attach itself to ongoing institutions. If it failed, the traditional procedures remained with little harm done.

The more conservative approach to enhancing the operation of existing institutions nevertheless had important consequences for the process and results of decisions reached in the League, and these were perceived by the participants. As the sentiments of the local grass-roots chapters became more articulate, organized, and coalesced, the chapters were able to develop highly focused plans for influencing the subsequent state convention. The visibility of the gap between local sentiment and state leaders also increased. As a result, the final outcome of the state convention was given a new "tilt." The game had not changed: the traditional institutions and rules were still in existence. Yet the relative strength of the forces was different.

At the conclusion of our experiment, the participants had designed new uses for the conference network. The local leaders, either in writing to others or over the conference network, expressed the desire to use it again between the biannual conventions to inform one another of local developments. Second, all of the local chapters have identical committees in charge of pursuing specific missions, such as financing or welfare reform; and local committee chairmen hope to use a future conference network to coordinate local efforts and share experiences.

The enthusiastic response of the League to the conference network experiment suggests that in the future it would be better to design citizen technologies initially as adjuncts to existing institutions. Over time, the users probably will design their own uses for the technology; as experience is gained and trust in the technology develops, certain traditional and very costly political technologies may be replaced, such as state conventions that require members to travel hundreds of miles. But it would seem best for this to emerge slowly through trial and error rather than as the starting point.

SIZE, TIME, AND INEQUALITY

In light of the classical constraints on democracy, it is clear that the model of citizen technology tested in the League offers only partial solutions. The electronic conference calls did lessen the impact of geographic size by making it easy and cheap for the local presidents to communicate with one another. The technology also ameliorated the problem of time: by using the home telephone circuits the participants did not have to travel to a meeting, and perhaps stay away from their families overnight. And, as we described at length above, the technology did have the effect of weakening the power of the state leadership vis-a-vis local chapters.

Yet several other dimensions of the classical constraints were not solved at all. The problem of demographic size—which means not all can participate at once, or all cannot speak to all—was solved by limiting participation to the 96 local presidents, who were treated as representatives of the larger membership. There is not technological solution to the problem of demographic size. With direct participation limited, inequality inherently arises. In our League experiment, we sought to lessen inequality between the state leadership and local chapters. But this leaves out of the picture the problems of the ordinary League member who was not aided by the technology directly. As we suggested in Chapter 3, inequality at this level cannot now be technologically redressed without at the same time altering the conception of democracy toward a plebescitarian-totalitarian model.

Hence, the interactive technology tested here—and other interactive technologies which are likely to arrive shortly, like two-way cable television—do not offer instant solutions to the very old problems of size and inequality. They may very well—if organized properly—contribute to the amelioration of some problems faced by a democracy, such as geographic size, time, and inequality between institutionalized power blocs and grass-roots groups that are well organized, active, and intensely interested. This is no mean accomplishment.

But other questions arise. How might such a technology be used by a real and much larger polity like a city or town? Is it realistic to believe that in the United States of the 1980s there will be much demand for a citizen technology?

5

OTHER APPLICATIONS:
A FANTASY

Extending our research results to larger political settings forces us to consider two kinds of problems. The first is political: where would a citizen technology be used, and who would actually use it? The second is organizational and more technical: how could a larger political unit of 100,000 people, for instance, use a system such as that developed in the previous chapter? Following the principle that fantasy is more pleasant than reality, let us dream that the political problems have been solved and look first at the organizational and technical possibilities. We will return to reality in the next chapter. Here we want to outline an application for two cities each with a population of 100,000 persons, of whom 50,000 citizens of voting age.

One city, it is assumed, is a low-density, suburban community, while the other is a high-density, urban community where everyone lives in high-rise apartment buildings. As we shall see, each city produces different cost and organizational possibilities. While no real city is either all suburban or all high-rise, urban in character, the examples provide polar estimates. In each case, let us assume a city of this size is attempting to decide among various plans of solid waste disposal.

Figure 3 presents a model for a suburban city in which it is assumed there are approximately 20 single-family homes to a city block, each with two adults. The model has four levels: block, neighborhood, community, and city-wide. The consensus-building process would begin with a priming event, most likely the results of a study by the city planning department or county auditor of the various options for solid waste collection and disposal, and various funding alternatives. This event could be broadcast over a local radio or television station, or alternatively, be part of a mailing to city residents. After priming, the experts

FIGURE 3

Model For a Suburban City

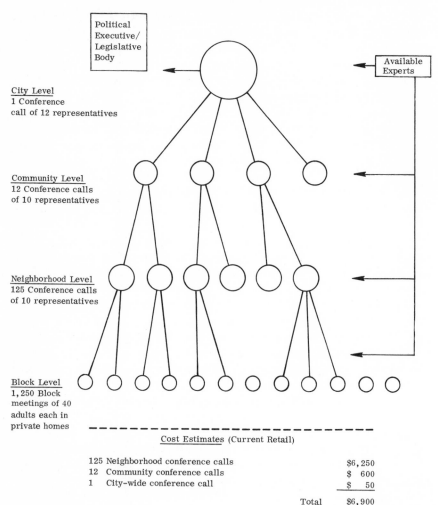

Cost Estimates (Current Retail)

125	Neighborhood conference calls	$6,250
12	Community conference calls	$ 600
1	City-wide conference call	$ 50
	Total	$6,900

Source: Compiled by the author.

remain on call to city residents at any level of the process. In a decision such as solid waste disposal, where the options and costs are relatively easily modeled, the experts could be asked by citizens to use an interactive computer model to test out various plans and proposals.

Once primed, the consensus-building process begins at the block level: a private home in each block is used for a meeting of the 40 block adults to discuss the issues, to use the phone to contact the experts, and eventually to decide on a single most desired option, or perhaps a rank order of their preferences. Each block meeting selects a person to represent the block at the next higher neighborhood level.

In the same home in which the block meeting has developed a rank order of preferences, after perhaps an hour or so of conversation, a prearranged conference network is established, connecting the block representatives in groups of ten in accordance with their proximity to one another. Other persons at the block meeting can listen as their representative argues for the position of his block. This conference call could take an hour or much less, depending on the amount of disagreement.

We are now in the second hour of the process. Each neighborhood conference call selects over the phone a representative. This is then connected into a community conference-call network combining the representatives of neighborhoods into 12 conference calls of ten persons each. This community-level conference call could take place in the same home as the block meetings and neighborhood calls, or it could take place at a later time. In any event, we are now in the third hour of the process.

Each of the community conference calls selects one representative, who is subsequently connected into a city-wide conference network of city-wide differences, and either decides on a single option or established an order of preferences by rank. Once again, as at all levels, a group of experts is on call to answer factual questions and provide estimates. It is now the end of the fourth hour.

The articulation of the consensus-building process with the political executive and legislature is left purposely vague at this point. Several options are open. The entire list of alternatives could be voted on by all adults through a brief reestablishment of the conference network, mail-in ballots, or automated call-in circuits in which citizen votes could be tabulated by a polling device. This vote could be used to establish an order by rank of citizen preferences. Alternatively, the city-level conference network, composed of 12 community representatives, could decide which solutions are preferred and so inform the executive. Or the city-level conference could (by previous changes in the city charter) force a vote on the city council. The nature of the articulation can and should vary with circumstances, the most important of which seems to be the desires of the citizens. If they have sufficient trust in the conference-call network, they may not believe that a final vote of all citizens is necessary or that forcing the executive and legislature is desirable.

Should elected officials decide to ignore the results of the conference network, the citizens have a recourse: the network can be reestablished to discuss plans for organizing the electoral defeat of the executive and certain legislators. Briefly, the conference network can be used not only to advise but also to punish. Moreover, the existence and use of the network does not depend on the whims and wishes of the political structure.

The cost of a single run for a suburban city for the telephone circuits is approximately $7,000. It is expected, however, that these retail prices of 1977 can be substantially reduced by wholesale block buying of phone time and technological changes in the switching system (outlined above). Efficiencies could reduce the cost by a factor of 10 to $700 per run.

The costs in a high-rise city are much lower because of the greater densities and the resultant ease of organizing face-to-face meetings within buildings. A model for such a city is represented in Figure 4; current cost estimates for this model are $650.

Quite clearly both of these models are to some extent unrealistic. A city of 100,000 citizens is most likely a combination of both high-rise and horizontal development. Cities of this size are usually heterogeneous with respect to social class, ethnicity, and religion. Although blocks and neighborhoods, floors, and buildings, are usually homogeneous, communities and cities are not. Insofar as most important public issues affect groups differentially, it may be necessary and desirable to organize conference networks in such a manner as to take into account the different citizen subgroups. For instance, in some cities it might be desirable to organize conference networks along ethnic lines, with the groups bargaining with one another only at the highest city-wide level. In this manner each group can determine collectively its best interests without interference. But these questions only raise technical-organizational problems; in principle the technology is quite flexible.

The nature of the feedback links to citizens is more problematic. It is desirable for the citizen to know the nature of the deliberations at each level, and to know how his representatives are bargaining. In our models the citizen is physically present in the first two levels: he directly participates in the block meetings, and he listens in on neighborhood conference call meetings. The citizen is not present at the community and city-wide levels. The city-wide meeting of 12 representatives could easily be broadcast on television or radio. The 12 community meetings could be handled in several ways. Each of the 125 community representatives could inform by phone the neighborhood level, and by word of mouth the nature of community-level decisions could be spread. Alternatively, if the city were wired for cable TV, each of the 12 community level meetings could be assinged a channel and the citizen could listen in. On the other hand, the average citizen may trust his representative and the process sufficiently as desire not to feedback from the community level meetings.

Finally, it may be the case that several runs are needed on very controversial issues. The decisions of higher levels in the process may produce new

FIGURE 4

Model for a High-Rise City

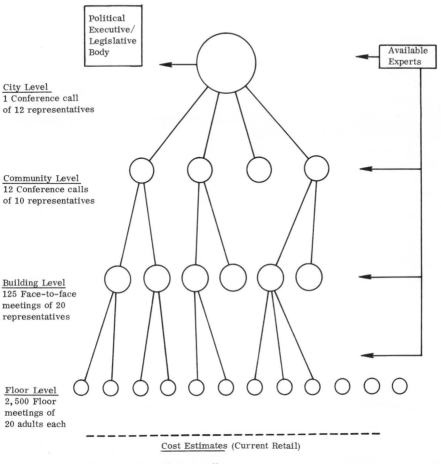

City Level
1 Conference call
of 12 representatives

Community Level
12 Conference calls
of 10 representatives

Building Level
125 Face-to-face
meetings of 20
representatives

Floor Level
2,500 Floor
meetings of
20 adults each

Cost Estimates (Current Retail)

12 Community conference calls $600
1   City-wide conference calls $ 50
                              Total $650

Source: Compiled by the author.

information or new positions which the average citizen should consider. In this case, two or three runs on consecutive Sunday forenoons should provide more than sufficient feedback and participation opportunities. On many issues, however, there is probably not enough citizen interest to support several runs.

It is conceivable, then, that with communities of up to perhaps 100,000 persons the kind of citizen technology tested with the League could be organized for a relatively small cost. In much larger communities the design becomes more cumbersome: additional levels of telephone conferencing have to be added on. On the basis of using groups of 30 citizens, and taking advantage of the exponential nature of a telephone-conference tree, six levels of conference calling would be sufficient to encompass 198 million persons. Yet, clearly, the task of organizing theses levels becomes unmanageable with such larger numbers: it is currently inconceivable that AT&T could provide sufficient conference bridges, let alone operator assistance.

In a practical, organizational sense, the kind of citizen technology outlined here is realizable in large organization and political units of about 100,000 maximum size. Even in these settings, however, the alignment of political forces and trends does not augur well for citizen technology.

6

REALISTIC
PROSPECTS FOR
CITIZEN
TECHNOLOGY

If we leave the world of futurist fantasy and consider the realistic prospects for citizen technology, we are immediately confronted by some nasty
facts and troublesome questions. Given the nature of the corporate giants who
control the present and future development of technology, what kind of citizen
technology are we likely to get? In the world of organizations, from Chicago's
Democratic machine, to organized labor and business, to Friends of the Earth,
is there a demand at any price for more democracy? Who would want or benefit
from citizen technology?

The answers to these questions are, in part, conditional upon the recognition of certain facts. First, it is apparent that technology cannot overcome the
limitations that are found in a democracy and are imposed by size, time, and
political inequality. Plans and experiments in mass-participation technology,
national electronic town halls, and national plebiscites threaten the end of
democracy, not the renewal. It is clear that the answer to the problem of political participation—and the larger problem of institutional legitimacy—is not
the packaging of television programs, opinion polls, or opening the studios to
"the people," who are defined differently from day to day. Rather, the answer
lies in somehow developing participatory methods that increase the deliberative
and organizational power of the citizenry vis-a-vis the corporate and governmental gargantua that dominates political life.

The League experiment demonstrates that it is possible to ameliorate the
consequences of large size, limited time commitments, and political inequality
while still maintaining a democratic structure. This is possible when democracy
is conceived as an organization of power in which many groups compete for
political influence in legitimate ways. The interactive technology acts under
these conditions as a useful tool for expediting the process of deliberation and

the emerging of political consensus and organized coalitions. Even under these conditions, several observations highlight the limitations of technology for enhancing democracy.

COMMUNITY AND TELECOMMUNICATIONS

Contrary to the early speculations of McLuhan and others that new communications technology would generate new communities, most research concerned with increasing citizen participation through technology has found that citizens are generally uninterested in participating, even with new technology. For this reason, it is unrealistic to expect than any citizen technology—even mass-participatory devices—will result in drastic increases in participation or political interest. The experience of the New York Regional Plan Association "Choices for '76" effort is instructive. This $2 million experiment in mass participation for a metropolitan region of 20 million persons, utilizing five planning films broadcast over 18 television stations and summarized in six major newspapers, produced the following response: an average of 600,000 households of the region's 8 million viewed the films (7.5 percent of the 8 million households); about 25,000 persons participated in at least one discussion group (0.25 percent of the region's adults); about 132,500 voting ballots were returned (3 percent of the 2.5 million ballots distributed). An evaluation of the effort by the Regional Plan Association concluded that "those who took the trouble to fill out and deposit the ballots had far more education and income than the region's residents as a whole, and white suburbanites were overrepresented."[1] The persons who participated in this experiment by viewing, balloting, and in a few instances, speaking, were drawn largely from the politically active and interested segments of the population. Political activism and interest precedes and largely determines the consequences of the technology. Put differently, utilization of new participatory technology tends to reflect the political community. In this sense, new technology cannot be expected to build political communities where none existed before.

In our experiment with the League, it is quite clear that the fact that the League existed for nearly 50 years, and that its members are self-selected by virtue of their interest in political matters, accounts in part for the enthusiastic reception and success of our experiment. Other research with cable television at the Center For Policy Research would support the notion that a technological assist to citizen participation works best where there is a preexisting, organized, social community. One cable TV experiment that compared electronic town hall meetings in two adjacent apartment buildings, one with a tenants association and the other without, found that use of the participatory technology in the "active" building was twice that in the "atomized," unorganized building.[2]

It is difficult to know with the same degree of certainty what the long-term effects of citizen technology might be. The same research cited above holds some hope that participation might increase slightly even among the nonactive and uninterested. In the case of the cable TV apartment house experiment above, participation increased among tenants in both kinds of buildings—the organized and unorganized. Interest in collective issues also increased among both types. The problem of course, is that the organized tenants responded much more favorably to the new participation techniques. We shall return to the implications of this later.

CONSENSUS AND CONFLICT

A related problem of community-technology interface concerns the impact of participatory technology upon levels of conflict and consensus. One criticism of our research would be that similar findings could not be produced elsewhere, for several reasons. First, the League is a highly consensual, homogeneous organization whose members are educated and wealthy. Second, applications in more cleavage-ridden organizations and politics would either smear over existing cleavages or be destroyed in the political fray. Moreover, the whole emphasis upon consensus ignores the more common phenomenon of social contradictions, conflict, and cleavage. Let us look at these criticisms more closely.

The focus in the League experiment upon consensus among local chapters may tend to obscure the whole point of the exercise, which was to heighten and equalize political conflict between local chapters and the larger state organization. The most important social conflict in the League appeared to us to be between the local chapters and a growing, more powerful state leadership. Necessary to a fair and adequate joining of this conflict was the mobilization of heretofore isolated local chapters into more powerful coalitions. Briefly, meaningful conflict among groups in large organizations and nations requires consensus within major subgroups as to the nature of the issues. Otherwise we would be left with the babble of millions of voices and the joining of no conflicts.

More to the point, however, is that the League is quite similar in many respects to other private associations and organizations. Most voluntary associations and subgroups in industrial societies are highly homogeneous with respect to social class, religion, and/or ethnicity. This is true of unions, police benevolent associations, and church groups. In this respect, the League of Women Voters is not unusual. Second, most of these groups are highly consensusal with respect to the underlying principles and raison d'etre of the group. Cleavages within groups usually follow age, skill, and political ideology lines and usually involve tactical differences. Moreover, the pluralist citizen technology used in the League experiment can be organized along such cleavage lines.

For example, consider the case of a union in which cleavages have led to the development of an institutionalized party system in which various groups compete for elective offices. Rather than establish a single electronic network which might tend to ignore existing cleavages, it is possible to develop multiple networks which operate within the context and under the control of the major parties. Here the technology would work to build consensus *within* major subgroups; consensus *among* the major subgroups could be developed at a traditional convention or within some other conflict-resolving institution.

Hence, in many respects, the League is not far different from thousands of other associations in the United States; and in those respects in which it is different, the technology is flexible enough to accomodate these differences.

POLITICAL INEQUALITY

A more vexing aspect of the relationship between new participatory technology and political communities concerns the impact of the technology on inequality. In Chapter 3 we distinguished between social inequality (unequal distributions of money, education, and status) and political inequality (unequal distribution of political power). Although the two are often related, it is also clear from the experience of many societies that several hundred million social equals do not inevitably lead to political equality. Differences in personal values and political skills, as well as the dynamics of large-scale organization, produce political stratification which is nearly impossible to mandate away. The appearance of a new political resource in the form of citizen technology— regardless of how it is organized or what technology is used—is likely to be utilized by the most politically skilled and organized groups in the population. The experience of previous information technology in education and management illustrates that the gap between the powerful and weak is enhanced by these innovations.

The problem is not simply that corporate giants like General Motors (GM) or International Telephone and Telegraph (ITT) will be able to use citizen technology for their own ends to the disadvantage of less powerful groups of citizens. Indeed, they would in a free society be allowed to use the new devices. But the fact is that these powerful institutions (including federal and state governments) already possess and utilize conference-call networks and videoconference networks for corporate decision making and management training. The more widespread distribution of such technology to the larger population is of no immediate benefit to them (unless, of course, the technology is organized in such a fashion as to provide them with a large, captive audience, which we discuss below).

The deeper problem caused by any citizen technology is its potential for increasing the gap between the small group of active citizens (about 10 to 15 percent of the U.S. voting age population) and inactive citizens. The League experiment showed that a citizen technology could transform a social aggregate of potential political activism into an acting political coalition (what Marx called the transition from a class *an sich* to a class *für sich*). Yet the technology was not designed in that experiment to accomplish the same for ordinary local chapter members. Relative to the heightened political influence of the local chapter presidents, we must assume the political influence of the ordinary member probably declined. Even if ordinary citizens were allowed to participate actively with a citizen technology as discussed in Chapter 5, it is only the most interested and active among them who would participate. The experience of the Regional Plan Association in New York simply confirms this; new advances in participatory methods will activate only those who are already politically aware, interested, and relatively more powerful.

The problem of political inequality potentially increasing under the influence of new communications technology becomes more severe as it is realized that important interests in a plural society are not represented or organized. Ethnic minorities, the poor, most of the elderly, small rural farmers, and so forth are represented in the political process only by very weak organizations, if at all. As the apartment house experiments illustrated, new participatory technologies will produce the greatest gains for those already organized. This is especially true with the kind of interactive citizen technology developed for the League. While not as difficult to use as a computer, the interactive technologies require some financial resources and, more important, a measure of organizational structure and skill.

The kind of interactive citizen technology outlined in earlier chapters appears, then, to be capable of equalizing political competition between organized subgroups and a central leadership or institution. This is no mean accomplishment, and at least is an advance over the mass-participation schemes and experiments, which do not seem to increase anyone's influence except that of the elite that controls the central studio or data-processing center. Nevertheless, the other aspects of the problem of political inequality—such as including the now inactive segments of the population—are likely to be unaffected and perhaps exacerbated by new telecommunications technology.

IS THERE A DEMAND FOR DEMOCRACY?

The value attached to the democratic process varies considerably among societies, even those labeled as Western democracies. Within each of these societies it is clear that a citizen technology would work to enhance the political process only in certain social settings. That is, the groups and associations that comprise the fabric of social life are more open to certain kinds of new information technologies than to others. The key to this puzzle involves the linkage or fit between the social function of the organization and the nature of the technology.

When we think of modern organizations, the most common image is that of a large bureaucracy—either private or public—whose principal mission is the maximization of a limited rationality or getting the biggest bang for the buck. Labor unions seeking a larger wage, corporations more profit, government agencies efficiency in the management of public affairs, and political parties a larger vote come to mind. The strength of these organizations lies in specialization, a division of labor, hierarchy, and limited, utilitarian commitments of employees.

The idea of democratizing these organizations has always come up against the counterargument, in the United States as well as in Europe, that such experimentation would interfere with efficient production or the attainment of organizational goals. Empirical research on the question of whether modern organizations can be run effectively as democracies is mixed: in some instances productivity goes up, in others down. There is no solid evidence that happy democratic workers produce more, and thus the reservations of corporations in the United States are probably justified. In Sweden, on the other hand, the argument has gone beyond productivity to the issue of legitimate representation of interests. In the words of Stig Gustafsson, the general counsel of white collar workers in Sweden, the worker who spends a large part of his life in the corporation "has an interest in the enterprise's being run in a sensible manner, and he feels a responsibility for this. He needs the right of codetermination."[3]

Yet in the United States these ideas remain largely foreign to both business and labor. The use of new information technology in these organizations principally involves the use of computers to collect, store, process, and distribute information among various levels of hierarchy and expertise. Use of participatory technology in such organizations would seem to require major institutional change and recognition of different values.

A very different kind of organization appears at first glance to provide a natural ground for the use of citizen technology. These we might call "movement organizations" whose principal function appears to be maximizing intense personal involvement of members in service to some goal. Student movements, the civil rights movement, and religious cults are examples of such organizations. These organizations are strong for reasons quite different from bureaucracies. There tends to be little specialization, expertise, or hierarchy among the brotherhood of members. At times there seems to be little organization per se, but instead a plethora of thousands of isolated groups linked only by the tenuous threads of shared values and purpose. Commitments of members are total, intereactions and recruitment are face to face, and the ethos focuses on direct action.

While it is conceivable that some movement organizations might be interested in using citizen technology to better coordinate the actions of dispersed-movement cells, it would seem that much of the spontaneity of movements would be lost. As one of the strengths of dispersed-movement organizations is their ability to confound social control agencies by acting in an uncoordinated fashion on many fronts, use of sophisticated citizen technology would open up the possibility of greater surveillance by authorities. Moreover, the neatly structured interplay of plural groups which is embodied in the design of an interactive citizen technology does not fit easily into the political culture of movements that tend to emphasize ideological certainty, intense involvement, and personal witness to the faith. Cool and dispassionate deliberation has never been a forte of social movements. A more natural kind of information technology for social movements would be what we have called mass-participation technology, like television, radio, and printed media—all of which can function to communicate the ideas, beliefs, and actions of disparate cells from one to another. Even here the technology is a poor substitute for the drama of actually participating in a movement event like a march, demonstration, or rally.

A somewhat less typical kind of organization which nevertheless is becoming increasingly common does provide a more suitable home for the kind of citizen technology we have outlined. These organizations might be called "umbrella organizations" because they typically are composed of hundreds of smaller, local organizations. Many of the larger, more established civil rights groups like the National Association for the Advancement of Colored People (NAACP) are composed of local and state organizations; certain labor unions are composed of relatively autonomous local chapters; some city and state organizations like the Greater Detroit movement are similarly composed of groups representing a broad spectrum of the population. In some states that have referendum procedures which allow organized citizens to place legislation directly before the voters in the form of propositions, such as California, Colorado, and Wisconsin, the formation of large, statewide, ad hoc umbrella groups is common. In California, the Coastal Plan Committee, which successfully lobbied the electorate to support a very strong coastal land-planning measure, was itself composed of over 1,000 local groups. A more recent group is the "Yes on Proposition 15 Committee," which is coordinating the efforts of the Sierra Club, Friends of the Earth, and 500 other local conservation groups toward passage of a bill limiting nuclear energy plants in California.

Typical of the opposition that popularly based umbrella groups face is the "No on Proposition 15 Committee," composed of public utility corporations, engineering and construction firms who have begun a $3 million campaign to defeat the proposition (this is compared to the $300,000 budget of the umbrella organization).   The industry group has hired several prominent physicists, writers, and former politicans to speak in favor of atomic power, and has begun distributing 10 million copies of a tabloid extolling the benefits of atomic power. In the words of the "Yes" committee, "They've got the money and we've got to get the people, organize in every county, ring every doorbell— direct voter contact."[4]

Umbrella organizations differ considerably from either movements or pure bureaucracies. They tend to be single-issue groups concerned with limited political objectives; they are clearly less structured than a formal bureaucracy, but more organized than a pure social movement. They tend to fall in between movements and bureaucracies in terms of hierarchy, specialization, and division of labor. Perhaps the most interesting feature of such groups is that they are strong only insofar as they reflect the sentiments of their constituent organizations, which contribute to the maintenance of the umbrella organization with personnel and money. In short, umbrella organizations have a more clear, vested interest in internal democracy and the representation of constituent interests.

The social and political role of such groups is not especially well documented or understood. In referendum states they have often been successful in circumventing the pervasive penetration of the political structure by corporate and labor interests, which dominate both political parties in several states. In states without the referendum, umbrella groups have been successful in coordinated lobbying efforts of legislators, the hiring of experts, and the dissemination of information to the public. In this sense, popularly based umbrella organizations can and often do function as effective counterweights to the influence of peak associations of business and labor.

Yet, just as often such umbrella groups taste defeat; in the competition against vested-interest group alignments they simply lack the political resources and skills. The problems are much more complex than mere differentials in money. In the case of the popular-based "Yes on Proposition 15 Committee" noted above, their problem is the organization of local chapters in over 30 disparate counties. Success here depends upon tailoring the overall message (oppose more atomic development) to the specific characteristics of local communities that may be composed of ranchers, farmers, fruit growers, or urbanites. Unless one can count on Divine Providence to coordinate such efforts, a great deal of communication is required among such local chapters and between local organizations and the coordinating committee in order to discuss how such tailoring is to proceed, to distribute resources where needed, and to evaluate the success or failure of various tactics. Typically, umbrella groups lack the technological tools and organizational skills necessary to the effort.

It would seem then that within the organizational world of complex societies the demand for more democracy—and the tools that might enhance its operation—are rather limited. In the case of bureaucratic organizations, major structural changes would be required in addition to reevaluation of the managerial ethos. While it is possible that the radical mayors of Berkeley, California, or Madison, Wisconsin, would condone the use of citizen technology in their political organization, most U.S. cities and counties are motivated by different political images, such as the current fascination with computers and the use of big business methods like the city manager form of government. Experiments in democracy and participation—as the 1950s showed—are likely to bring forth all sorts of citizen demands and make public a great deal of dissatisfaction. Quite naturally, the politicians and bureaucrats who survived the 1960s in the United States are prone in the 1970s to look toward better accounting methods as the fount of progress, not toward citizen technology.

For very different reasons, there will also be little future demand for citizen technology among the various movement organizations likely to appear in the future, of either a political or religious character. The logic of the interactive citizen technology we have outlined maximizes opportunities for deliberation and compromise in order to form larger coalitions. This may be a virtue in some settings, but seems out of place in movement organizations given to ideological purity, intense devotion, and faith. However, those movements that survive the transition from movement to stable organization—like many of the national civil rights organizations—increasingly will find themselves in a position to use effectively new technological innovations.

Political pundits have long since buried the student and civil rights movement activists of the 1960s. The most popular Sunday magazine version of this ritual concerns these activists who have taken up with religious cults. Yet in fact the student activists did not disappear. Rather, they grew up, and a good many of them found new, more sophisticated settings for political activity. Many are to be found today in the infrastructure of populist groups ranging from the reform wing of traditional political parties to ecology groups, consumer action groups, antinuclear power groups, insurgent professional groups, and the like. Such umbrella groups with a popular base are increasingly common and politically important at least in the United States. They have the minimal organizational requisites and skills to utilize the kind of citizen technology we have outlined, as well as the structural and cultural requisites for internal democracy that the technology presupposes. It is among these groups, then, that the initial demand for a citizen technology is to be found. Simple interactive devices—like telephone conference circuits—could be used and controlled by these groups without significant expenditures. Moreover, it is unnecessary to hire a consultant firm, or a computer firm, to design such a system. No elite carriers of the technology are required and no permanent investments are needed.

WHAT KIND OF CITIZEN TECHNOLOGY ARE WE LIKELY TO GET?

The demand for interactive citizen technology designed for the League and recommended above for populist groups is relatively small. Only a few such groups exist in each state, and they are composed of a small percentage of the politically active population. Briefly, there is no mass market for the kind of citizen technology we have outlined. It is unlikely, then, that large corporations will put resources into the development of devices required for an authentic citizen technology. In this sense, citizen technology is quite different from computers, pocket calculators, one-way cable television, home television videotape machines, and citizen's band radio. Each of these technologies center about costs of production and other technical matters. The corporate giants that will produce new technology in the 1980s are likely, then, to place their research and development dollars here rather than experiment with citizen technology as we have outlined.

All of this suggests, then, that the kind of citizen technology likely to be developed in the next decade will not be like the interactive devices we have discussed. Instead they will be ersatz versions attached to very profitable mass-participation media. Quite simply, there is corporate and political profit to be made from large captive audience. Attached to the devices that produce such audiences will be procedures and perhaps little black boxes designed to allow the citizen to select his preference on national issues, send a message to the sponsor (approve or don't approve), or to "let the government know what he thinks." As we were treated to headlines in the early 1960s that read COMPUTERS JOIN WAR ON CRIME, so in the early 1980s we will learn that CABLE TV AIDS DEMOCRACY, and during the half-time of the Superbowl, an important national issue will be discussed by 12 experts, followed by a vote of the national audience, the results of which will be sent to Congress and the president. Depending upon the average distance between the television room and the refreshments, several million persons will punch questionnaires, call a station, or push a button on a little black box. To the unaware citizen this may seem at first glance a useful development. The growing recognition that the little black boxes are not connected to anything of importance, however, will only worsen and complicate the sense of alienation from U.S. institutions.

If this vision sounds Orwellian, that is because it is Orwellian. More worrisome than its literary origin is the recognition that it is the most likely path of development for future citizen technology in the United States. I believe these false versions of citizen technology must be resisted. In the next decade, corporate and government experiments and projects will be announced, testing the value of technological enhancements to democracy. It is to be hoped that this book will contribute to a critical awareness of the limitations and dangers that certain technologies portend for democracy.

NOTES

1. *Listening to the Metropolis; An Evaluation of the New York Region's "Choices for '76" Mass Media Town Meetings* (New York: Regional Plan Association, Inc., 1974).

2. Robert Zussman and Nancy Castleman, "Politics and Electricity: Can an Electronic Town Hall Meeting Work?" (New York: Center for Policy Research, Inc., 1972).

3. "To Swedish Labor, Equality Is Being Boss," New York *Times*, April 7, 1976.

4. "Coast Unit Fights Nuclear Curbs," New York *Times*, April 11, 1976.

KENNETH C. LAUDON is Associate Professor of Sociology at John Jay College (CUNY) and Senior Research Associate at the Center For Policy Research, New York City. Professor Laudon's interests lie in the fields of complex organization, telecommunications and computer technology, and politics. He is the author of *Computers and Bureaucratic Reform* and has contributed articles and reviews to *Science*, *Datamation*, and the *American Journal of Sociology*.

CITIZENS' GROUPS AND BROADCASTING
                    Daniel L. Guimary

ORAL HISTORY PROGRAM MANUAL
                    William W. Moss

PUBLIC ACCESS CABLE TELEVISION IN THE UNITED
STATES AND CANADA: With An Annotated Bibliography
                    Gilbert Gillespie

THE VIDEO TELEPHONE: Impact of a New Era in Telecommunications A Preliminary Technology Assessment
                    Edward M. Dickson
                    in association with Raymond Bowers